Disclaimer: The information contained in this book is based on the experience and research of the author. It is not intended as a substitute for consulting with your physician or other health-care provider. Any attempt to diagnose and treat an illness should be done under the direction of a health-care professional. The publisher and author are not responsible for any adverse effects or consequences resulting from the use of any of the suggestions, preparations, or procedures discussed in this book.

Some of the recipes in this book include raw eggs, meat, or fish. When these foods are consumed raw, there is always the risk that bacteria, which is killed by proper cooking, may be present. For this reason, when se1ving these foods raw, always buy certified salmonella -free eggs and the freshest n1eat and fish available fron1a reliable grocer, storing them in the refrigerator until they are se1ved. Because of the health risks associated with the consumption of bacteria that can be present in raw eggs, meat, and fish, these foods should not be consumed by infants, small children, pregnant women, the elderly, or any persons who may be immunocompromised. The author and publisher expressly disclaim responsibility for any adverse effects that may result from the use or application of the recipes and information contained in this book.

CONTENTS

INTRODUCTION

There's nothing quite like a barbecue on a sunny day, is there? I have to say that a wood pellet smoker and grill took my outdoor cooking to the next level. If you're a fan of throwing some steaks on the grill, then you probably know that coal or gas often leads to food ending up a bit more charred than you wanted. If you don't pay attention to the food and turn it frequently, you may end up ordering take-out for dinner. Well, with a wood pellet smoker and grill, you can relax and spend some time with your family away from the heat.

But it's more than that. If you're looking for an appliance that is convenient and versatile, then a wood pellet grill, such as Traeger Grill, is the way to go.

You may be asking yourself, "But, how would you know? Isn't your husband the one who does the grilling?" Well, he was our barbecue frontman! That was until I discovered just how easy (and fun) it was to do it myself! All you do is put your meat on, set the temperature, and enjoy a drink while you relax with your feet up.

When it comes to versatility, a wood pellet grill does more than barbecue. You can use it to smoke, roast, braise, and, believe it or not, bake! If you're as adventurous as I am, you'll be attempting to bake a cheesecake in your griller in no time!

It's worth mentioning that a wood pellet smoker and grill will leave a more significant dent in your bank account than a charcoal or gas grill would. That being said, it is absolutely worth it, if you ask me.

I am so excited about this outdoor cooking appliance that I decided to write a cookbook to convince readers who aren't sure about making this investment that it is indeed worth it. Of course, I didn't forget about those of you who already have a wood pellet smoker and grill, and you're just looking for some delicious recipes to try out! Before we jump into the recipes, let's first cover the basics of wood pellet smokers and how to use them to get yourself the title of Barbecue Master.

CHAPTER 1: THE WOOD PELLET SMOKER AND GRILL BASICS

The Structure and Component

When you first look at your wood pellet grill's inner workings, you may feel somewhat overwhelmed. It has a few components that all work together and make the appliance such a winner.

Hopper: This is the part of the machine you will fill with hardwood pellets.

Auger: This is the component that transports the pellets to the firepot. Think of it as the motor of your wood pellet grill.

Firepot: The area below the grill where the actual fire will be.

Hot rod (igniter element): After the auger moves the wood pellets into the firepot, the hot rod will ignite, and the fire will start.

Induction fan: The fan will stoke the fire and turn your wood pellet smoker into something similar to a traditional convection oven.

Resistance temperature detector (RTD): This device will measure the temperature in your wood pellet grill and smoker. RTDs are more accurate than the previously used thermocouples, but they're more fragile, and you should be careful when moving your grill.

Heat deflector: This part of your wood pellet grill and smoker provides a barrier between the food and flames. The heat deflector is a plate that is designed to fit over the firepot and prevent charring and burning by redirecting the heat. It turns your grill into a wood-fired convection oven.

Flame zone pan: If you want to grill at high temperatures without a barrier in between the flame and food, you'll use this component in conjunction with searing grates and griddle accessories.

Grease bucket: The grease bucket will catch any fat or liquid and stop it from falling into the flames. How much grease it collects depends on if you trimmed the fat from the meat you're cooking. I recommend you line your grease bucket with foil to make the clean-up less of a hassle.

Why Choose a Wood Pellet Smoker and Grill?

We've already covered the convenience and versatility that comes with a wood pellet smoker, but this appliance will give you the best-tasting, moist food you'll ever eat. I am not exaggerating. Furthermore, your smoker is straightforward to operate and maintain. The main thing you have to do is make sure the hopper is filled with wood pellets, that it is plugged into a power source, and you're ready to get cooking! With other smoker-grills, you'll have to monitor the unit to keep the temperature steady. This is unnecessary when you have a wood pellet smoker and grill since they are specifically designed to maintain the temperature at set guidelines.

One of the things I like most about my wood pellet smoker and grill is its ability to maintain a temperature that is low enough to get the maximum smoke taste! The consensus is that to smoke protein, the meat's surface temperature should be below 140 degrees Fahrenheit, something you can easily achieve with a wood pellet smoker.

The fuel efficiency of wood pellet grills is also worth a mention. When you power up the fan, you turn your wood pellet griller into an outside convection oven, which means you'll end up using a fraction of the wood chips than you would use for charcoal or gas grills.

Lastly, the fact that a wood pellet grill is so easy to clean was a big selling point for me. I don't want to spend a lot of time cleaning after a barbecue with the family. Before we invested in a wood pellet grill, we had a charcoal smoker, and it was a mess to clean. The wood pellet grill requires minimal cleaning after each use — it's not even necessary to empty the firepot every time.

How To Use Your Wood Pellet Grill and Smoker

When you get your wood pellet grill, there are a few things you'll have to do before first use. Firstly, some wood pellet grills require assembly unless you ask your dealer to do it for you. But don't worry, it's not a difficult task. I won't say that it is something I could handle alone, you know I needed my husband's muscles, but the instructions were easy to follow. We were done in less than an hour and ready for the initial burn-in.

Burn-in Procedure

Manufacturers recommend that you give your grill a "dry run" before actually using it to cook food for the first time. The reasoning behind this is to burn off any contaminants or chemicals used during the manufacturing process. All you have to do is fill the hopper with wood pellets as well as half a handful in the firepot. Plug in the appliance and turn it on. Set the temperature to between 350 and 450 degrees Fahrenheit and let it run for up to 60 minutes. Check the owner's manual for the recommended temperature and time.

This process is usually adequate, but you will find that some manufacturers recommend you season your grill as an additional step.

Seasoning Your Grill

If you want your wood pellet grill to give its best performance, "seasoning the grill," as the pros call it, is your ticket to mouth-watering meals. It's a straightforward process: Cook a pound of bacon at 350 degrees Fahrenheit for an hour. After you're done, your smoker will be seasoned, and you can invite the neighbors over for a barbecue.

What About Hot Spots?

It will take a few practices runs for you to cook some of the most delicious meals, you and your family will ever enjoy. As with any new appliance, you have to get to know the ropes before having enough confidence to really push the limits. That being said, not all wood pellet grills and smokers are created equal. This is why I suggest you test your grill's surface temperatures for constant heat and hotspots.

The easiest way to do this is with the biscuit test. Get your hands on some refrigerator biscuits and line them in the corners, front, rear, and center of the wood pellet grill. Follow the cooking instructions for the biscuits. When done, you will be able to tell where the grill gets hotter and where the cooler spots are. From then on, you can pack your food according to this information.

However, if you're more technical-minded, you can use a remote temperature probe to test the temperatures on various places in the grill.

Keeping Your Grill Clean

If you keep your wood pellet smoker clean, your food will be infused with clean smoke every time. It only takes a few minutes and will ensure you get the best out of your appliance with each use. The most important thing to do is to replace the foil on the grease drip pan. You don't have to do it after cooking food for a short time — you can use it two to four short times before changing the foil. However, if something requires an above-average cooking time, replace the foil straight after. Of course, this is presuming that you use foil at all (more on this later). If you do not use foil, scrape off any food residue from the drip pan as often as you can. You don't want the fumes from old grease to burn off at a high temperature when you're cooking something fresh.

Use a wire brush to clean the grill grates while they're still hot, and then use a warm cloth or paper towel to wipe down the sides. Then, when the pit is fully cooled, you can remove the drip pan and spray it with a degreaser to clean thoroughly. Remove any ashes from the firepot and body of the grill. If you let ash pile up, it will reduce the efficiency of your grill by preventing the igniter rod from kindling the pellets at the start-up.

For me, it makes more sense to cover the drip pan in foil. This makes cleaning even less effortless — no elbow grease needed to scrape off any food particles. Furthermore, by using clean foil, the food I'm cooking is not subjected to any fumes given off when caked-on residue burns off. I always like to start with a nice and clean drip pan.

Food-grade Wood Pellets

When you buy wood pellets for your grill, you should get food-grade barbecue wood pellets. The product is controlled from start to finish to ensure that it doesn't get contaminated with harmful chemicals or foreign pollutants. These pellets contain no additives except for vegetable oils added during the process, which means they will burn cleanly and leave extremely little ash. Food-grade chips are cylindrical, about ¼-inch wide, and made out of compressed hardwood sawdust. The raw material is sourced directly from fruit orchards.

The chips usually have a combination of flavors but are either oak- or alder-based. The manufacturer determines percentages. Where some manufacturers will use 75 percent base wood with 25 percent flavor hardwood mixed in, others may opt for a higher flavor percentage. You will also get flavors like apple, maple, and hickory that contain no base wood. I'll give you more about the various wood pellet flavors and food combinations in the next section, but first, let's discuss how you should store your chips.

Each type of wood has a distinct flavor that goes with certain types of meat. Pairing wood pellets with a specific food is based on a spectrum from mild to intense smoking results. Here are some everyday pairings and what flavors you can expect.

Alder: It has a mild sweet taste and aroma that goes well with salmon and other fish, beef, pork, fish, poultry, and lamb.

Apple: This is the strongest fruitwood and also the most popular. It goes well with pork, lamb, poultry, and game meats.

Cherry: If you're looking for a slightly sweet flavor, then cherry wood is what you're looking for. It will give a rosy tint to meats that may end up looking like the meat is not cooked properly. That's only true for the untrained eye, of course. Pair cherry chips with beef, pork, poultry, and game.

Hickory: The most commonly used wood pellets. It has a strong bacon-flavored taste that goes well with all meats.

Maple: Tangy, mild, and sweet. Goes well with beef, pork, and poultry.

Mesquite: Strong, spicy, and tangy flavor. Adds a distinct taste to all types of meat, but it doesn't pair well with fish.

Oak: It has a milder taste than hickory but is stronger than fruitwoods. Use it with beef and fish.

Pecan: These wood chips have a spicy, nutty flavor that works well with beef, pork, and poultry.

Wood Pellet Storage

Keeping your wood pellets dry is the most critical consideration when it comes to choosing a container or space to store the chips. Should your pellets get wet from absorbing too much moisture or standing outside in the elements for too long, they will break down and won't perform up to standards. There is even a chance that they could jam and damage your grill's auger.

After opening a bag of wood pellets, store the remaining in a wood pellet dispenser, or if you still have your charcoal dispenser, it will work just as well. A trash can, pet food container, or an air-tight plastic bucket will also work. As an extra measure, put the box in your garage or a dry shed.

Cooking Tips and Tricks

Before we get to the importance of quality meat and seasoning, let's look at the recommended minimum internal temperatures. It is safest to cook all foods to these temperatures as measured before removing the meat from the heat source — use a digital food thermometer. That being said, there is nothing wrong with cooking food at a higher temperature. It's all about personal preference.

• Beef, pork, lamb, and veal steaks, chops, and roasts should be cooked at 145 degrees Fahrenheit. Meat should rest at least three minutes.

• Poultry, it doesn't matter what cut, should be cooked at 165 degrees Fahrenheit.

• Fish and shellfish should be cooked at 145 degrees Fahrenheit.

Now that you know what temperature you should aim for, another vital aspect to consider when it comes to cooking on a wood pellet grill and smoker is the quality of the meat and the seasoning. I recommend checking out a few local butcher shops and selecting the one with the best quality. If your meat is of a high standard, your job is halfway done.

Secondly, seasoning is important. You don't want it to overpower the meat, but it should instead interact with the natural flavors of the food you're cooking. The right spice can push the "wow factor" of your cooking off the charts. I like to use a trusty old all-purpose seasoning, but nothing is stopping you from mixing your own combination of spices and flavors. Just make sure you end up with seasoning that works well with the wood pellet grill and smoker — low-and-slow cooking and smoking. Experiment to find a real crowd-pleaser.

How to Use FTC

In this cookbook, you will see 'FTC' resting mentioned with some recipes. This acronym stands for 'foil-towel-cooler' and indicates that meats should be rested before serving. The reason for holding or resting meat is to redistribute the juices into the meat. Making use of the FTC method will produce moist and tender cuts of meat. Professionals, caterers, pitmasters, and chefs may use an industrial unit called a Cambro to achieve such juicy results. But, the "poor man's Cambro" works just as well. All you have to do is double-wrap the cooked meat in heavy-duty foil to contain the juice. Next, wrap the foiled meat in a towel and then place it in a cooler. You can fill the rest of the cooler with towels to keep the heat from escaping too fast. How long you FTC meat depends on what cut it is. For example, pork butts and briskets will be sealed for a minimum of two hours but can be kept in the cooler for up to six. Just be careful when you do remove the meat from the cooler. It may still be very hot.

Indirect and Direct Cooking

Your wood pellet grill/smoker is primarily designed for indirect cooking. This is when the heat is deflected away from food and allows it to cook slowly and evenly. I mentioned the heat deflector earlier when we looked at the various components of your wood pellet smoker. This stainless-steel plate makes it possible for meat to be kept out of direct contact with open flames. Instead, the heat is radiated out and around the food like in a traditional convection oven. It will take longer to cook, but it will be done more evenly. Direct cooking, as you can imagine, means direct heat is used for cooking the food. The cooking time is shorter, which means the smoke infusion won't be that strong. You'll get those classic grill marks, but not much of the woody taste.

Manufacturers are starting to see that offering an indirect and direct cooking setup in one appliance is the way to go. They now provide the flexibility to select which cooking method you prefer without having to change the configuration.

Still, most wood pellet grills and smoker recipes in this book call for indirect setup, so use your drip pan as per the user manual.

If you do want to play around with a direct setup, you may need to replace your drip pan with a direct pan. Some units may also require you to move cover plates around to make it direct-cooking compatible. The best way to tell if your wood pellet grill and smoker is set up for indirect or direct cooking is to look at the pan. A solid pan is for indirect cooking, and one with open holes is for the direct method. I recommend you get searing grates for direct cooking as they will provide better searing results.

There you have it — everything you need to know about using your wood pellet grill and smoker. Now you're ready to jump into the recipes and get crowned your neighborhood's Barbecue Master.

CHAPTER 2: VEGETABLES AND SIDES

Cabbage Slaw with Carrot

Prep time: 15 minutes | Cook time: 10 to 15 minutes | Serves 4 to 6

1 small or ½ large green cabbage (about 1 pound / 454 g), quartered and cored

1 small onion, peeled and quartered

2 carrots, trimmed and peeled

2 ribs celery, trimmed

1 apple, peeled, quartered, and cored

½ cup mayonnaise or smoked mayonnaise

3 tablespoons cider vinegar, or to taste

3 tablespoons sugar

1 tablespoon prepared horseradish (don't drain)

½ teaspoon celery seeds, or to taste

Coarse salt (sea or kosher) and freshly ground black pepper, to taste

1. Set up your smoker following the manufacturer's instructions and preheat to 225ºF (107ºC). Add the wood as specified by the manufacturer.

2. Thinly shred the cabbage, onion, carrots, celery, and apple on a mandoline, in a food processor fitted with a slicing or shredding disk, or with a chef's knife. Spread out the vegetables and apple in a thin layer in 2 aluminum foil pans.

3. Place the vegetables in their foil pans in the smoker and smoke until lightly bronzed with smoke, but still raw, 10 to 15 minutes. Do not overcook. Let the vegetables cool to room temperature.

4. While the vegetables are cooling, make the dressing: Combine the mayonnaise, vinegar, sugar, horseradish, celery seeds, and salt and pepper to taste in a large bowl and whisk until the sugar is dissolved.

5. Stir the vegetables into the dressing. Correct the seasoning, adding salt or vinegar as desired; the slaw should be highly seasoned. Cover the slaw and refrigerate until serving. Try to serve within a couple of hours of mixing.

Potato Salad with Mayo

Prep time: 30 minutes | Cook time: 1 to 1½ hours | Serves 4 to 6

2 pounds (907 g) boiling potatoes (preferably organic), scrubbed with a stiff brush

2 tablespoons extra virgin olive oil

Coarse salt (sea or kosher) and freshly ground black pepper, to taste

½ cup mayonnaise or smoked mayonnaise

3 tablespoons Dijon mustard

1 tablespoon red wine vinegar, or more to taste

2 hard-cooked eggs, peeled and coarsely chopped

2 tablespoons chopped fresh dill

2 scallions, trimmed, white parts minced, green parts thinly sliced crosswise

8 pitted green olives or pimiento-stuffed olives, thinly sliced or coarsely chopped

8 cornichons (tiny tart French pickles) or 1 dill pickle, coarsely chopped (about 3 tablespoons)

1 tablespoon drained capers, or to taste

Spanish smoked paprika (pimentón), for sprinkling

1. Cut any larger potatoes in half or quarters; leave small ones whole. The idea is for all the pieces to be bite size, about 1 inch across. Arrange the potatoes in a single layer in an aluminum foil pan. Stir in the olive oil and season with salt and pepper.

2. Set up your smoker following the manufacturer's instructions and preheat to 275ºF

(135ºC). Add wood as specified by the manufacturer.

3. Place the potatoes in the smoker and smoke until tender (a bamboo skewer will pierce the spuds easily), 1 to 1½ hours, or as needed. Stir a couple of times so the potatoes brown evenly. Remove the potatoes and let cool slightly (they should be warm).

4. While the potatoes smoke, make the dressing: Combine the mayonnaise, mustard, and vinegar in a large bowl and whisk to mix. Whisk in the chopped eggs, dill, scallions, olives, pickles, and capers. Cover and refrigerate until the potatoes are ready.

5. Stir the warm potatoes into the dressing. Correct the seasoning, adding salt, pepper, and vinegar to taste; the salad should be highly seasoned. You can serve the potato salad warm or chilled (cover and refrigerate, or quick-chill the salad over a bowl of ice). Transfer to a serving bowl and dust with smoked paprika before serving.

Cheesy Potato with Bacon

Prep time: 15 minutes | Cook time: 1 hour | Serves 4

4 large baking potatoes (12 to 14 ounces / 340 to 397 g each—preferably organic)

1½ tablespoons bacon fat or butter, melted, or extra virgin olive oil

Coarse salt (sea or kosher) and freshly ground black pepper, to taste

4 strips artisanal bacon (like Nueske's or the home-smoked bacon here), cut crosswise into ¼-inch slivers

6 tablespoons (¾ stick) cold unsalted butter, thinly sliced

2 scallions, trimmed, white and green parts finely chopped (about 4 tablespoons)

2 cups coarsely grated smoked or regular white Cheddar cheese (about 8 ounces / 227 g)

½ cup sour cream

Spanish smoked paprika (pimentón) or sweet paprika, for sprinkling

1. Set up your smoker following the manufacturer's instructions and preheat to 400ºF (204ºC). Add enough wood for 1 hour of smoking as specified by the manufacturer.

2. Scrub the potatoes on all sides with a vegetable brush. Rinse well under cold running water and blot dry with paper towels. Prick each potato several times with a fork (this keeps the spud from exploding and facilitates the smoke absorption). Brush or rub the potato on all sides with the bacon fat and season generously with salt and pepper.

3. Place the potatoes on the smoker rack. Smoke until the skins are crisp and the potatoes are tender in the center (they'll be easy to pierce with a slender metal skewer), about 1 hour.

4. Meanwhile, place the bacon in a cold skillet and fry over medium heat until browned and crisp, 3 to 4 minutes. Drain off the bacon fat (save the fat for future potatoes).

5. Transfer the potatoes to a cutting board and let cool slightly. Cut each potato in half lengthwise. Using a spoon, scrape out most of the potato flesh, leaving a ¼-inch-thick shell. (It's easier to scoop the potatoes when warm.) Cut the potato flesh into ½-inch dice and place in a bowl.

6. Add the bacon, 4 tablespoons of the butter, the scallions, and cheese to the potato flesh and gently stir to mix. Stir in the sour cream and salt and pepper to taste; the mixture should be highly

seasoned. Stir as little and as gently as possible so as to leave some texture to the potatoes.

7. Spoon the potato mixture back into the potato shells, mounding it in the center. Top each potato half with a thin slice of the remaining butter and sprinkle with paprika. The potatoes can be prepared up to 24 hours ahead to this stage, covered, and refrigerated.

8. Just before serving, preheat your smoker to 400ºF (204ºC). Add enough wood for 30 minutes of smoking. Place the potatoes in a shallow aluminum foil pan and re-smoke them until browned and bubbling, 15 to 20 minutes. Or you can heat them in a 400ºF (204ºC) oven.

Root Vegetable Hash Browns

Prep time: 15 minutes | Cook time: 40 to 60 minutes | Serves 2 to 3

2 pounds (907 g) root vegetables (I like to use a combination of Yukon Gold potatoes, sweet potatoes, and carrots)

1 medium-size onion, peeled

2 tablespoons extra virgin olive oil, plus extra as needed

Coarse salt (sea or kosher) and freshly ground black pepper, to taste

2 teaspoons Spanish smoked paprika (pimentón; optional)

1 tablespoon butter

1. Rinse the root vegetables, scrubbing them with a stiff brush, and blot dry with paper towels. I leave the peel intact; you may need to trim away any blemishes. Cut the vegetables, including the onion, into ½-inch dice.

2. Place all the vegetables in a 10-inch cast-iron skillet or large aluminum foil pan, spreading them out in a single layer. Drizzle with olive oil and stir to mix. Season generously with salt and pepper and the paprika, if using, and stir again to mix. Add the butter.

3. Set up your grill for indirect grilling and heat to medium-high 400ºF (204ºC). Place the pan with the vegetables on the grill grate away from the heat. Toss the wood chunks or chips on the coals.

4. Cover the grill and smoke-roast the hash browns, stirring occasionally with tongs so they cook evenly, until browned and crisp, 40 to 60 minutes. If they start to dry out, add a little more oil. Serve directly from the skillet or pan.

Creamed Corn

Prep time: 30 minutes | Cook time: 30 to 40 minutes | Serves 4 to 6

The Smoked Vegetables:

4 ears fresh sweet corn, husks and silk removed, or 3 cups frounceen corn kernels, thawed

1 small onion, peeled and quartered

2 tablespoons (¼ stick) butter, melted

Coarse salt (sea or kosher) and freshly ground black pepper, to taste

1 poblano pepper, stemmed, cut in half lengthwise, and seeded

The Creamed Corn:

1 tablespoon butter

1 tablespoon unbleached all-purpose flour

2 teaspoons Spanish smoked paprika (pimentón) or sweet paprika

½ cup dark beer

1 to 1½ cups half-and-half

1 tablespoon light or dark brown sugar

1½ cups coarsely grated Cheddar cheese

1. Set up your smoker following the manufacturer's instructions and preheat to 225ºF (107ºC) to 250ºF (121ºC). Add the wood as specified by the manufacturer.

2. Lightly brush the corn and onion with the butter and season with salt and pepper. Place the corn, onion, and poblano pepper on the smoker rack and smoke until lightly bronzed with smoke, 30 to 40 minutes. Transfer to a cutting board and let cool. Cut the kernels off the cobs. Cut the onion and poblano into ¼-inch dice.

3. Melt the butter in a large saucepan over medium heat. Stir in the vegetables and cook until sizzling, 3 minutes. Stir in the flour and paprika and cook for 1 minute. Stir in the beer, increase the heat to medium-high, and boil for 1 minute (to cook off the alcohol). Stir in 1 cup half-and-half and the brown sugar and boil until thickened, 1 minute.

4. Reduce the heat and gently simmer the corn until thick and richly flavored, 5 to 8 minutes, stirring often. Stir in the cheese and cook just long enough to melt it. If the mixture seems too thick, add more half-and-half. Add salt, pepper, and additional sugar, if desired, and serve.

Onion with Bacon and Cheese

Prep time: 20 minutes | Cook time: 2½ to 3 hours | Makes 4 onions

4 large (12- to 14-ounces / 340- to 397-g each) sweet onions, peeled

3 tablespoons unsalted butter

4 strips artisanal bacon (like Nueske's or the Made-from-Scratch Bacon here), cut crosswise into ¼-inch slivers

4 jalapeño peppers, seeded and diced (for spicier onions, leave the seeds in)

½ cup barbecue sauce (use your favorite)

½ cup grated Cheddar or pepper Jack cheese (optional)

1. Using a sharp paring knife and starting at the top (opposite the root), cut an inverted cone-shaped cavity about 2 inches across the top and 2 inches deep in each onion. (The core should come out in a cone-shaped plug.) Chop the pieces you remove.

2. Melt 1 tablespoon of the butter in a medium-size skillet. Add the chopped onion, bacon, and jalapeños and cook over medium heat, stirring occasionally, until lightly browned, 4 minutes. Place a spoonful of the filling in the cavity of each onion. Divide the remaining 2 tablespoons of butter into 4 pats and place one on top of each onion. (The onions can be prepared several hours ahead to this stage. Place them on a plate, cover with plastic wrap, and refrigerate.)

3. Set up your smoker following the manufacturer's instructions and preheat to 225ºF (107ºC) to 250ºF (121ºC). Add the wood as specified by the manufacturer.

4. Place the onions on grill rings or in a shallow aluminum foil pan. Smoke until gently yielding when squeezed on the sides, about 2 hours.

5. Place 2 tablespoons of the barbecue sauce on each onion and top with 2 tablespoons of the cheese, if using. Continue smoking the onions for another 30 to 60 minutes. To test for doneness, squeeze the sides of the onion—they should be soft and easy to pierce with a metal skewer. Transfer the onions to a platter or plates for serving.

Mushroom and Pecan Bread Pudding

Prep time: 30 minutes | Cook time: 1 hour | Serves 8

1 loaf (1 pound / 454 g) day-old brioche, cut into 1-inch cubes (8 to 10 cups)

12 ounces (340 g) mixed exotic mushrooms

6 tablespoons (¾ stick) unsalted butter

1 bunch scallions, trimmed, white and light green parts thinly sliced

1 rib celery, trimmed and chopped (optional)

8 fresh sage leaves, thinly slivered

1 cup coarsely chopped pecans or peeled roasted chestnuts

¼ cup Cognac or bourbon (optional)

5 large eggs (preferably organic)

3 cups heavy (whipping) cream

¼ teaspoon freshly grated nutmeg, or to taste

½ teaspoon coarse salt (sea or kosher), or to taste

½ teaspoon freshly ground black pepper, or to taste

1. Set up your grill for indirect grilling and preheat to medium 350ºF (177ºC).

2. Arrange the brioche chunks in a single layer in a large aluminum foil pan. Place the pan on the grill grate away from the heat and cover the grill. For even more smoke flavor, add wood chunks or handfuls of wood chips to the coals. Indirect-grill the brioche, stirring occasionally so the cubes brown evenly, until toasted and golden brown, about 15 minutes. Set the pan of brioche aside to cool.

3. Meanwhile, trim the ends off the mushroom stems; remove and discard the stems if using shiitakes. Wipe the mushrooms clean with a damp paper towel. Cut large mushrooms into ¼-inch slices; leave small ones whole.

4. Melt 3 tablespoons of the butter in a 12-inch cast-iron skillet on the stove or grill side burner over medium-high heat. Add the scallions, celery, if using, and sage and cook, stirring often, until golden brown, 4 minutes. Add the mushrooms and pecans. Increase the heat to high and cook, stirring often, until the mushrooms brown and all their liquid evaporates, 5 minutes. Add the Cognac, if using, and boil until only 2 tablespoons of liquid remain, 2 minutes. Remove from the heat and let cool slightly.

5. Crack the eggs into a large bowl and whisk until smooth. Whisk in the cream. Stir in the mushroom mixture, then the brioche cubes. Grate in the nutmeg and stir in salt and pepper; the mixture should be highly seasoned. Spoon it back into the skillet and top with the remaining 3 tablespoons butter, cut into thin slices. (The pudding can be prepared several hours ahead to this stage; cover with plastic wrap or aluminum foil and refrigerate, if you have room. But the texture will be better if you cook it right away.)

6. If you shut down the grill after toasting the brioche, fire it up again for indirect grilling and preheat to 350ºF (177ºC). Add the wood chunks or chips to the coals following the manufacturer's instructions. Cover the grill and smoke-roast the pudding until puffed and browned on top and cooked through (a skewer inserted into the center should come out clean), about 45 minutes.

7. Serve it right from the skillet. Even more reason to give thanks for Thanksgiving.

Beans with Bacon

Prep time: 20 minutes | Cook time: 2 to 2½ hours | Serves 6 to 8

6 slices (6 ounces / 170 g) artisanal bacon, cut crosswise into ¼-inch slivers

1 medium-size onion, peeled and finely chopped (about 1½ cups)

1 poblano pepper, stemmed, seeded, and diced

3 cans (15 ounces / 425 g each) cooked beans, drained, rinsed, and drained again

¼ cup packed dark brown sugar, plus extra as needed

¼ cup molasses, or to taste

¼ cup barbecue sauce (use your favorite)

¼ cup ketchup

2 tablespoons Worcestershire sauce

1 tablespoon Dijon mustard

2 tablespoons cider vinegar, plus extra as needed

½ teaspoon liquid smoke (optional; no need to add it if you smoke the beans)

Coarse salt (sea or kosher) and freshly ground black pepper, to taste

1. Cook the bacon in a heavy pot or Dutch oven over medium heat to render the fat, about 5 minutes. Spoon out and discard all but 2 tablespoons of the fat.

2. Add the onion and poblano to the bacon and cook, stirring often, until lightly browned, 5 minutes. Stir in the beans, sugar, molasses, barbecue sauce, ketchup, Worcestershire, mustard, vinegar, and liquid smoke, if using. Add salt and pepper to taste.

3. Set up your smoker following the manufacturer's instructions and preheat to 225ºF (107ºC) to 250ºF (121ºC). Add the wood as specified by the manufacturer.

4. Smoke the beans, uncovered, until thick and richly flavored, 2 to 2½ hours, or as needed, stirring from time to time so the mixture cooks evenly. If the beans start to dry out, stir in 1 cup of water, and cover the pot. Adjust the seasoning before serving, adding salt, sugar, and vinegar to taste.

Mayo and Cheese Stuffed Pear Salad

Prep time: 10 minutes | Cook time: 0 minutes | Serves 6

1 (16-ounce / 454-g) can pear halves, drained

¼ cup mayonnaise

¼ cup shredded sharp Cheddar cheese

6 cherries, fresh (pitted) or maraschino

12 to 18 large iceberg lettuce leaves, rinsed and dried

1. Place pear halves, cut side up, on a plate. Spoon about 2 teaspoons of the mayonnaise into the cavity of each pear. Sprinkle the cheese over the mayonnaise. Top each one with a cherry. Chill the pears, covered, for at least 3 hours.

2. To serve, arrange 2 to 3 lettuce leaves on a plate and place the pear halves on top of them.

Beans with Peach

Prep time: 20 minutes | Cook time: 4 hours | Serves 8

2 pounds (907 g) (about 4 cups) dried navy or great northern beans

¼ cup (packed) light brown sugar

Salt and freshly ground black pepper, to taste

¼ cup prepared mustard

¼ cup maple syrup

½ cup ketchup

3 cups canned peach pie filling

1 (7-ounce / 198-g) jar diced pimento peppers, drained

1. Place the beans in a large nonreactive bowl, and add enough cold water to cover them by 3 to 4 inches. Cover the bowl loosely with a kitchen towel and leave the beans to soak at room temperature overnight.

2. When you are ready to cook the beans, rinse them thoroughly in fresh cold water, and drain.

3. Place the beans in a large pot, and add water to cover. Bring to a boil, reduce the heat, and simmer for 1 hour. Drain the beans.

4. Preheat a smoker or oven to 300ºF (149ºC).

5. In a large bowl, combine the brown sugar, salt and pepper, mustard, maple syrup, ketchup, pie filling, and peppers. Mix well. Then add the beans and stir again. Pour the bean mixture into

a large aluminum pan (for the smoker) or into a large ovenproof baking dish or Dutch oven. (You can assemble the beans to this point 1 day ahead; cover and refrigerate until you're ready to cook them.)

6. Add just enough water to the pan to cover everything, and cover the pan with aluminum foil. Cook in the smoker or oven until the beans are tender, about 4 hours, checking hourly to make sure they aren't drying out (if they are, add more water to the pan). The beans are done when the top is dark brown and bubbling. If you want the top to be slightly crunchy, uncover the pan for the last 30 minutes of cooking.

7. Let the beans stand for about 15 minutes, then serve.

Creamy Potato Salad with Mayo

Prep time: 15 minutes | Cook time: 15 to 20 minutes | Serves 8

2 pounds (907 g) red-skinned new potatoes

1 cup sour cream

1 teaspoon dried dill weed

½ teaspoon garlic powder

½ teaspoon onion powder

⅓ cup chopped fresh chives

1 cup mayonnaise

1 tablespoon coarsely ground black pepper

1 tablespoon salt

6 hard-boiled eggs, chopped

Basic barbecue rub, for garnish (optional)

1. Wash the potatoes well. In a large heavy pot, bring water to a boil. Add the potatoes and boil for 15 to 20 minutes, or until they are tender, being careful not to overcook them, as you don't want them mushy.

2. Drain the potatoes in a colander, and run cold water over them to stop them from continuing to cook. Let them cool in the colander.

3. Slice the potatoes into thin rounds, leaving the skin on. Set aside.

4. In a medium bowl, combine the sour cream, dill, garlic powder, onion powder, chives, mayonnaise, pepper, and salt. Stir well.

5. In a large bowl, toss the potatoes with the chopped eggs and the sour cream dressing. Cover the bowl and chill in the refrigerator for 2 hours before serving. Sprinkle top with basic barbecue rub before serving, if desired.

Cabbage Slaw with Tomato

Prep time: 13 minutes | Cook time: 0 minutes | Serves 12

2 small heads green cabbage, coarsely chopped

2 medium sweet onions, diced

2 ripe tomatoes, diced

3 cups mayonnaise

Kosher salt, to taste

Freshly ground black pepper, to taste

Basic barbecue rub, optional

1. In a large bowl, combine the cabbage, onions, tomatoes, mayonnaise, salt, and pepper. Toss thoroughly. (You can prepare this up to 6 hours in advance and store it, covered, in the refrigerator. But if you do, do not add the salt until you're ready to serve the slaw, and toss it again just before serving; otherwise, the slaw becomes watery.) Garnish with basic barbecue rub, if desired.

2. Serve immediately.

Bacon Cornbread

Prep time: 10 minutes | Cook time: 20 to 25 minutes | Serves 6

1 cup all-purpose flour

1 cup yellow cornmeal

1 teaspoon salt

1 egg, beaten

1 cup milk

1 cup chopped crisp pork cracklin's or crumbled crisp bacon

1. Preheat the oven to 425ºF (218ºC).

2. In a large mixing bowl, sift the flour, cornmeal, and salt together until thoroughly combined. Add the egg and the milk, and mix until the batter is relatively smooth. Add the pork cracklin's. If the mixture seems too dry, add a tablespoon or two of water to moisten it.

3. Pour the batter into an 8-inch cast-iron skillet or an 8-inch square baking pan. Bake until the top is golden brown and a tester inserted into the middle of the cornbread comes out clean, 20 to 25 minutes.

4. Remove the cornbread from the oven and allow it to cool in the pan for 10 minutes before cutting and serving.

Potato and Pineapple Cheese Salad

Prep time: 13 minutes | Cook time: 0 minutes | Serves 6

1 head iceberg lettuce

6 slices bacon, cooked and chopped, or 1 (4.1-ounce / 116-g) can bacon bits

4 hard-boiled eggs, chopped

1 cup diced fresh pineapple, or 1 (8-ounce / 227-g) can pineapple niblets, drained

¼ cup chopped green onions (scallions), white and green parts

1 cup grated sharp Cheddar cheese

1 cup mayonnaise

1 cup sugar

1 cup canned or bagged shoestring potato sticks

¾ cup dried cranberries or cherries

1. Cut the head of lettuce into bite-size pieces.

2. In a large serving bowl, and in this order, layer the lettuce, chopped bacon, chopped eggs, pineapple, green onions, and cheese. Set aside.

3. In a small bowl, stir the mayonnaise and sugar together until well combined.

4. Drizzle the mayonnaise mixture over the salad. Scatter the potato sticks and cranberries on top of the dressing. Chill the salad, covered, for 1 hour before serving.

Smoked Okra

Prep time: 10 minutes | Cook time: 30 minutes | Serves 4

Nonstick cooking spray or butter, for greasing

1 pound (454 g) whole okra

2 tablespoons extra-virgin olive oil

2 teaspoons seasoned salt

2 teaspoons freshly ground black pepper

1. Supply your smoker with wood pellets and follow the manufacturer's specific start-up procedure. Preheat, with the lid closed, to 400ºF (204ºC). Alternatively, preheat your oven to 400ºF (204ºC).

2. Line a shallow rimmed baking pan with aluminum foil and coat with cooking spray.

3. Arrange the okra on the pan in a single layer. Drizzle with the olive oil, turning to coat. Season on all sides with the salt and pepper.

4. Place the baking pan on the grill grate, close the lid, and smoke for 30 minutes, or until crisp and slightly charred. Alternatively, roast in the oven for 30 minutes.

5. Serve hot.

Sweet Potato Chips

Prep time: 40 minutes | Cook time: 35 to 45 minutes | Serves 3

2 sweet potatoes

1 quart warm water

1 tablespoon cornstarch, plus 2 teaspoons

¼ cup extra-virgin olive oil

1 tablespoon salt

1 tablespoon packed brown sugar

1 teaspoon ground cinnamon

1 teaspoon freshly ground black pepper

½ teaspoon cayenne pepper

1. Using a mandolin, thinly slice the sweet potatoes.

2. Pour the warm water into a large bowl and add 1 tablespoon of cornstarch and the potato slices. Let soak for 15 to 20 minutes.

3. Supply your smoker with wood pellets and follow the manufacturer's specific start-up procedure. Preheat, with the lid closed, to 375ºF (191ºC).

4. Drain the potato slices, then arrange in a single layer on a perforated pizza pan or a baking sheet lined with aluminum foil. Brush the potato slices on both sides with the olive oil.

5. In a small bowl, whisk together the salt, brown sugar, cinnamon, black pepper, cayenne pepper, and the remaining 2 teaspoons of cornstarch. Sprinkle this seasoning blend on both sides of the potatoes.

6. Place the pan or baking sheet on the grill grate, close the lid, and smoke for 35 to 45 minutes, flipping after 20 minutes, until the chips curl up and become crispy.

7. Store in an airtight container.

Onion with Cheese

Prep time: 25 minutes | Cook time: 1 hour | Serves 6

Nonstick cooking spray or butter, for greasing

4 large Vidalia or other sweet onions

8 tablespoons (1 stick) unsalted butter, melted

4 chicken bouillon cubes

1 cup grated Parmesan cheese

1. Supply your smoker with wood pellets and follow the manufacturer's specific start-up procedure. Preheat, with the lid closed, to 350ºF (177ºC).

2. Coat a high-sided baking pan with cooking spray or butter.

3. Peel the onions and cut into quarters, separating into individual petals.

4. Spread the onions out in the prepared pan and pour the melted butter over them.

5. Crush the bouillon cubes and sprinkle over the buttery onion pieces, then top with the cheese.

6. Transfer the pan to the grill, close the lid, and smoke for 30 minutes.

7. Remove the pan from the grill, cover tightly with aluminum foil, and poke several holes all over to vent.

8. Place the pan back on the grill, close the lid, and smoke for an additional 30 to 45 minutes.

9. Uncover the onions, stir, and serve hot.

Squash with Butter

Prep time: 20 minutes | Cook time: 40 minutes | Serves 4

1 spaghetti squash

2 tablespoons extra-virgin olive oil

1 teaspoon salt

1 teaspoon freshly ground black pepper

2 teaspoons garlic powder

4 tablespoons (½ stick) unsalted butter

½ cup white wine

1 tablespoon minced garlic

2 teaspoons chopped fresh parsley

1 teaspoon red pepper flakes

½ teaspoon salt

½ teaspoon freshly ground black pepper

The Squash

1. Supply your smoker with wood pellets and follow the manufacturer's specific start-up procedure. Preheat, with the lid closed, to 375ºF (191ºC).

2. Cut off both ends of the squash, then cut it in half lengthwise. Scoop out and discard the seeds.

3. Rub the squash flesh well with the olive oil and sprinkle on the salt, pepper, and garlic powder.

4. Place the squash cut-side up on the grill grate, close the lid, and smoke for 40 minutes, or until tender

The Sauce

5. On the stove top, in a medium saucepan over medium heat, combine the butter, white wine, minced garlic, parsley, red pepper flakes, salt, and pepper, and cook for about 5 minutes, or until heated through. Reduce the heat to low and keep the sauce warm.

6. Remove the squash from the grill and let cool slightly before shredding the flesh with a fork; discard the skin.

7. Stir the shredded squash into the garlic-wine butter sauce and serve immediately.

Zucchini Squash Ratatouille Salad

Prep time: 15 minutes | Cook time: 25 minutes | Serves 6

1 whole sweet potato

1 whole red onion, diced

1 whole zucchini

1 whole squash

1 large tomato, diced

Vegetable oil, as needed

Salt and pepper, as needed

1. Preheat grill to high setting with the lid closed for 10-15 minutes.

2. Slice all vegetables to a ¼ inch thickness.

3. Lightly brush each vegetable with oil and season with Traeger's Veggie Shake or salt and pepper.

4. Place sweet potato, onion, zucchini, and squash on grill grate and grill for 20 minutes or until tender, turn halfway through.

5. Add tomato slices to the grill during the last 5 minutes of cooking time.

6. For presentation, alternate vegetables while layering them vertically. Enjoy!

Carrot with Fennel

Prep time: 10 minutes | Cook time: 45 minutes | Serves 8 to 12

1 pound (454 g) slender rainbow carrots

2 whole fennel, bupound

2 tablespoon extra-virgin olive oil

1 teaspoon salt

1 tablespoon fresh thyme

1. When ready to cook, set temperature to High and preheat, lid closed for 15 minutes. For optimal results, set to 500℉ if available.

2. Trim the carrot tops to 1-inch. Peel the carrots and halve any larger ones so they are all about ½-inch thick. Cut the fennel bupounds lengthwise into ½" thick slices.

3. Place the fennel and potato slices in a large mixing bowl. Drizzle with 2 tablespoons of the olive oil and a teaspoon of salt.

4. Toss to coat the vegetables evenly with the oil.

5. Place the carrots on a sheet pan. Drizzle with the additional 2 tablespoons of olive oil and a generous pinch of salt. Brush the olive oil over the carrots to distribute evenly.

6. Add the potatoes and fennel slices to the sheet pan. Nestle a few sprigs of herbs into the vegetables as well.

7. Place the pan directly on the grill grate and cook, stirring occasionally until the vegetables are browned and softened, about 35-45 minutes.

8. Allow to cool and serve with the Smoked Romesco Sauce. Enjoy!

Broccoli with Cheese

Prep time: 10 minutes | Cook time: 20 minutes | Serves 4

½ cup (120 ml) olive oil
½ cup (40 g) grated Parmesan cheese
1 tablespoon (10 g) garlic powder
1 teaspoon smoked paprika (optional)
1 teaspoon chili powder (optional)
Salt and pepper, to taste
1 large head broccoli (about 2 pounds / 907 g), stems removed, chopped into florets

1. Set your Traeger to run on HIGH.

2. In a large bowl, combine the olive oil, Parmesan cheese, garlic powder, paprika (if using), chili powder (if using), salt and pepper. Place the broccoli florets in the bowl and toss until evenly coated. Spread the broccoli on a sheet pan in a single layer, place in the smoker and close the lid.

3. After 10 minutes, flip the broccoli to crisp the other side. Close the lid and let the broccoli roast another 10 minutes or until both sides are slightly browned and crispy.

4. Serve warm.

CHAPTER 3: PORK

Pork Chops

Prep time: 10 minutes | Cook time: 55 minutes | Serves 4

4 (8-ounce / 227-g) pork chops, bone-in or boneless

Salt and freshly ground black pepper, to taste

1. Supply your smoker with wood pellets and follow the manufacturer's specific start-up procedure. Preheat the grill, with the lid closed, to 180ºF (82ºC).

2. Season the pork chops on both sides with salt and pepper.

3. Place the chops directly on the grill grate and smoke for 30 minutes.

4. Increase the grill's temperature to 350ºF (177ºC). Continue to cook the chops until their internal temperature reaches 145ºF (63ºC).

5. Remove the pork chops from the grill and let them rest for 5 minutes before serving.

Pork Tenderloin

Prep time: 15 minutes | Cook time: 4 or 5 hours | Serves 4 to 6

2 (1-pound / 454-g) pork tenderloins

1 batch Pork Rub

1. Supply your smoker with wood pellets and follow the manufacturer's specific start-up procedure. Preheat the grill, with the lid closed, to 180ºF (82ºC).

2. Generously season the tenderloins with the rub. Using your hands, work the rub into the meat.

3. Place the tenderloins directly on the grill grate and smoke for 4 or 5 hours, until their internal temperature reaches 145ºF (63ºC).

4. Remove the tenderloins from the grill and let them rest for 5 to 10 minutes before thinly slicing and serving.

Pork Tenderloin with Garlic

Prep time: 30 minutes | Cook time: 1½ to 2 hours | Serves 4 to 6

2 (1-pound / 454-g) pork tenderloins

1 batch Garlic and Soy Sauce Marinade

Smoked salt, to taste

1. In a large zip-top bag, combine the tenderloins and marinade. Seal the bag, turn to coat, and refrigerate the pork for at least 30 minutes.

2. Supply your smoker with wood pellets and follow the manufacturer's specific start-up procedure. Preheat the grill, with the lid closed, to 180ºF (82ºC).

3. Remove the tenderloins from the marinade and season them with smoked salt.

4. Place the tenderloins directly on the grill grate and smoke for 1 hour.

5. Increase the grill's temperature to 300ºF (149ºC) and continue to cook until the pork's internal temperature reaches 145ºF (63ºC).

6. Remove the tenderloins from the grill and let them rest for 5 to 10 minutes, before thinly slicing and serving.

Sweet and Spicy Pork

Prep time: 5 minutes | Cook time: 30 minutes | Serves 4 to 6

2 (1-pound / 454-g) pork tenderloins

1 batch Sweet and Spicy Rub

1. Supply your smoker with wood pellets and follow the manufacturer's specific start-up

procedure. Preheat the grill, with the lid closed, to 350ºF (177ºC).

2. Generously season the tenderloins with the rub. Using your hands, work the rub into the meat.

3. Place the tenderloins directly on the grill grate and smoke until their internal temperature reaches 145ºF (63ºC).

4. Remove the tenderloins from the grill and let them rest for 5 to 10 minutes, before thinly slicing and serving.

Honey Pork Belly

Prep time: 30 minutes | Cook time: 6 hours | Serves 8 to 10

1 (3-pound / 1.4-kg) skinless pork belly (if not already skinned, use a sharp boning knife to remove the skin from the belly), cut into 1½- to 2-inch cubes

1 batch Brown Sugar Rub

½ cup honey

1 cup Ketchup and BBQ Sauce

2 tablespoons light brown sugar

1. Supply your smoker with wood pellets and follow the manufacturer's specific start-up procedure. Preheat the grill, with the lid closed, to 250ºF (121ºC).

2. Generously season the pork belly cubes with the rub. Using your hands, work the rub into the meat.

3. Place the pork cubes directly on the grill grate and smoke until their internal temperature reaches 195ºF (91ºC).

4. Transfer the cubes from the grill to an aluminum pan. Add the honey, barbecue sauce, and brown sugar. Stir to combine and coat the pork.

5. Place the pan in the grill and smoke the pork for 1 hour, uncovered. Remove the pork from the grill and serve immediately.

Bacon Strips

Prep time: 5 minutes | Cook time: 20 to 30 minutes | Serves 4 to 6

1 (1-pound / 454-g) package thick-sliced bacon

1. Supply your smoker with wood pellets and follow the manufacturer's specific start-up procedure. Preheat the grill, with the lid closed, to 275ºF (135ºC).

2. Place the bacon strips directly on the grill grate, being careful they do not hang over the drain pan, and smoke for 20 to 30 minutes, or until done to your liking. Serve immediately.

Syrupy Bacon

Prep time: 15 minutes | Cook time: 2 hours | Serves 4 to 6

1 cup pure maple syrup

2 tablespoons honey

1 cup packed light brown sugar, divided

1 (1-pound / 454-g) package thick-sliced bacon

1. In a large airtight container, stir together the maple syrup, honey, and ½ cup of brown sugar until well mixed. Add the bacon and turn to coat. Cover the container and refrigerate overnight.

2. Supply your smoker with wood pellets and follow the manufacturer's specific start-up procedure. Preheat the grill, with the lid closed, to 200ºF (93ºC).

3. Remove the bacon from the marinade and place it directly on the grill grate, being careful it does not hang over the drain pan. Sprinkle with the remaining ½ cup of brown sugar. Smoke for about 2 hours, or until the bacon is cooked to your liking. Serve immediately.

Ham with Honey

Prep time: 20 minutes | Cook time: 4 or 5 hours | Serves 10 to 16

1 (5- or 6-pound / 2.3- or 2.7-kg) bone-in smoked ham

1 batch Cajun Rub

3 tablespoons honey

1. Supply your smoker with wood pellets and follow the manufacturer's specific start-up procedure. Preheat the grill, with the lid closed, to 225ºF (107ºC).

2. Generously season the ham with the rub and place it either in a pan or directly on the grill grate. Smoke it for 1 hour.

3. Drizzle the honey over the ham and continue to smoke it until the ham's internal temperature reaches 145ºF (63ºC).

4. Remove the ham from the grill and let it rest for 5 to 10 minutes, before thinly slicing and serving.

Ribs with Sauce

Prep time: 25 minutes | Cook time: 4 hours | Serves 4 to 6

2 (2- or 3-pound / 0.9- or 1.4-kg) racks baby back ribs

2 tablespoons yellow mustard

1 batch Brown Sugar Rub

½ cup plus 2 tablespoons maple syrup, divided

2 tablespoons light brown sugar

1 cup Pepsi or other non-diet cola

¼ cup Molasses BBQ Sauce

1. Supply your smoker with wood pellets and follow the manufacturer's specific start-up procedure. Preheat the grill, with the lid closed, to 180ºF (82ºC).

2. Remove the membrane from the backside of the ribs. This can be done by cutting just through the membrane in an X pattern and working a paper towel between the membrane and the ribs to pull it off.

3. Coat the ribs on both sides with mustard and season them with the rub. Using your hands, work the rub into the meat.

4. Place the ribs directly on the grill grate and smoke for 3 hours.

5. Remove the ribs from the grill and place them, bone-side up, on enough aluminum foil to wrap the ribs completely. Drizzle 2 tablespoons of maple syrup over the ribs and sprinkle them with 1 tablespoon of brown sugar. Flip the ribs and repeat the maple syrup and brown sugar application on the meat side.

6. Increase the grill's temperature to 300ºF (149ºC).

7. Fold in three sides of the foil around the ribs and add the cola. Fold in the last side, completely enclosing the ribs and liquid. Return the ribs to the grill and cook for 30 to 45 minutes.

8. Remove the ribs from the grill and unwrap them from the foil.

9. In a small bowl, stir together the barbecue sauce and remaining 6 tablespoons of maple syrup. Use this to baste the ribs. Return the ribs to the grill, without the foil, and cook for 15 minutes to caramelize the sauce.

10. Cut into individual ribs and serve immediately.

Ribs with BBQ Sauce

Prep time: 25 minutes | Cook time: 4 to 6 hours | Serves 4 to 8

2 (2- or 3-pound / 0.9- or 1.4-kg) racks spare ribs

2 tablespoons yellow mustard

1 batch Brown Sugar Rub

¼ cup Molasses BBQ Sauce

1. Supply your smoker with wood pellets and follow the manufacturer's specific start-up procedure. Preheat the grill, with the lid closed, to 225ºF (107ºC).

2. Remove the membrane from the backside of the ribs. This can be done by cutting just through the membrane in an X pattern and working a paper towel between the membrane and the ribs to pull it off.

3. Coat the ribs on both sides with mustard and season with the rub. Using your hands, work the rub into the meat.

4. Place the ribs directly on the grill grate and smoke until their internal temperature reaches between 190ºF (88ºC) and 200ºF (93ºC).

5. Baste both sides of the ribs with barbecue sauce.

6. Increase the grill's temperature to 300ºF (149ºC) and continue to cook the ribs for 15 minutes more.

7. Remove the racks from the grill, cut them into individual ribs, and serve immediately.

Cola Pork Ribs

Prep time: 25 minutes | Cook time: 4 hours | Serves 12 to 15

2 pounds (907 g) (907 g) country-style ribs

1 batch Brown Sugar Rub

2 tablespoons light brown sugar

1 cup Pepsi or other cola

¼ cup Molasses BBQ Sauce

1. Supply your smoker with wood pellets and follow the manufacturer's specific start-up procedure. Preheat the grill, with the lid closed, to 180ºF (82ºC).

2. Sprinkle the ribs with the rub and use your hands to work the rub into the meat.

3. Place the ribs directly on the grill grate and smoke for 3 hours.

4. Remove the ribs from the grill and place them on enough aluminum foil to wrap them completely. Dust the brown sugar over the ribs.

5. Increase the grill's temperature to 300ºF (149ºC).

6. Fold in three sides of the foil around the ribs and add the cola. Fold in the last side, completely enclosing the ribs and liquid. Return the ribs to the grill and cook for 45 minutes.

7. Remove the ribs from the foil and place them on the grill grate. Baste all sides of the ribs with barbecue sauce. Cook for 15 minutes more to caramelize the sauce.

8. Remove the ribs from the grill and serve immediately.

Paprika Pork Loin Roast

Prep time: 10 minutes | Cook time: 3 hours | Serves 8

¼ cup finely ground coffee

¼ cup paprika

¼ cup garlic powder

2 tablespoons chili powder

1 tablespoon packed light brown sugar

1 tablespoon ground allspice

1 tablespoon ground coriander

1 tablespoon freshly ground black pepper

2 teaspoons ground mustard

1½ teaspoons celery seeds

1 (1½- to 2-pound / 680- to 907-g) pork loin roast

1. Supply your smoker with wood pellets and follow the manufacturer's specific start-up procedure. Preheat, with the lid closed, to 250ºF (121ºC).

2.   In a small bowl, combine the ground coffee, paprika, garlic powder, chili powder, brown sugar, allspice, coriander, pepper, mustard, and celery seeds to create a rub, and generously apply it to the pork loin roast.

3.   Place the pork loin on the grill, fat-side up, close the lid, and roast for 3 hours, or until a meat thermometer inserted in the thickest part of the meat reads 160ºF (71ºC).

4.   Let the pork rest for 5 minutes before slicing and serving.

Pork and Pineapple Kebabs

Prep time: 20 minutes | Cook time: 1 to 4 hours | Serves 12 to 15

1 (20-ounce / 567-g) bottle hoisin sauce

½ cup Sriracha

¼ cup honey

¼ cup apple cider vinegar

2 tablespoons canola oil

2 teaspoons minced garlic

2 teaspoons onion powder

1 teaspoon ground ginger

1 teaspoon salt

1 teaspoon freshly ground black pepper

2 pounds (907 g) thick-cut pork chops or pork loin, cut into 2-inch cubes

10 ounces (284 g) fresh pineapple, cut into chunks

1 red onion, cut into wedges

1 bag mini sweet peppers, tops removed and seeded

12 metal or wooden skewers (soaked in water for 30 minutes if wooden)

1.   In a small bowl, stir together the hoisin, Sriracha, honey, vinegar, oil, minced garlic, onion powder, ginger, salt, and black pepper to create the marinade. Reserve ¼ cup for basting.

2.   Toss the pork cubes, pineapple chunks, onion wedges, and mini peppers in the remaining marinade. Cover and refrigerate for at least 1 hour or up to 4 hours.

3.   Supply your smoker with wood pellets and follow the manufacturer's specific start-up procedure. Preheat, with the lid closed, to 450ºF (232ºC).

4.   Remove the pork, pineapple, and veggies from the marinade; do not rinse. Discard the marinade.

5.   Use the double-skewer technique to assemble the kebabs. Thread each of 6 skewers with a piece of pork, a piece of pineapple, a piece of onion, and a sweet mini pepper, making sure that the skewer goes through the left side of the ingredients. Repeat the threading on each skewer two more times. Double-skewer the kebabs by sticking another 6 skewers through the right side of the ingredients.

6.   Place the kebabs directly on the grill, close the lid, and smoke for 10 to 12 minutes, turning once. They are done when a meat thermometer inserted in the pork reads 160ºF (71ºC).

Cheesy Bacon and Pork

Prep time: 25 minutes | Cook time: 2 hours 30 minutes | Serves 4 to 6

¼ cup yellow mustard

2 (1-pound / 454-g) pork tenderloins

¼ cup Pork Rub

8 ounces (227 g) cream cheese, softened

1 cup grated Cheddar cheese

1 tablespoon unsalted butter, melted

1 tablespoon minced garlic

2 jalapeño peppers, seeded and diced

1½ pounds (680 g) bacon

1. Slather the mustard all over the pork tenderloins, then sprinkle generously with the dry rub to coat the meat.

2. Supply your smoker with wood pellets and follow the manufacturer's specific start-up procedure. Preheat, with the lid closed, to 225ºF (107ºC).

3. Place the tenderloins directly on the grill, close the lid, and smoke for 2 hours.

4. Remove the pork from the grill and increase the temperature to 375ºF (191ºC).

5. In a small bowl, combine the cream cheese, Cheddar cheese, melted butter, garlic, and jalapeños.

6. Starting from the top, slice deeply along the center of each tenderloin end to end, creating a cavity.

7. Spread half of the cream cheese mixture in the cavity of one tenderloin. Repeat with the remaining mixture and the other piece of meat.

8. Securely wrap one tenderloin with half of the bacon. Repeat with the remaining bacon and the other piece of meat.

9. Transfer the bacon-wrapped tenderloins to the grill, close the lid, and smoke for about 30 minutes, or until a meat thermometer inserted in the thickest part of the meat reads 160ºF (71ºC) and the bacon is browned and cooked through.

10. Let the tenderloins rest for 5 to 10 minutes before slicing and serving.

Sauerkraut Apple with Pork

Prep time: 20 minutes | Cook time: 3 hours | Serves 8

1 (28-ounce / 794-g) jar or 2 (14½-ounce / 411-g) cans sauerkraut
3 Granny Smith apples, cored and chopped
¾ cup packed light brown sugar
3 tablespoons Greek seasoning
2 teaspoons dried basil leaves
Extra-virgin olive oil, for rubbing
1 (2- to 2½-pound / 0.9- to 1.1-kg) pork loin roast

1. Supply your smoker with wood pellets and follow the manufacturer's specific start-up procedure. Preheat, with the lid closed, to 250ºF (121ºC).

2. In a large bowl, stir together the sauerkraut, chopped apples, and brown sugar.

3. Spread the sauerkraut-apple mixture in the bottom of a 9-by-13-inch baking dish.

4. In a small bowl, mix together the Greek seasoning and dried basil for the rub.

5. Oil the pork roast and apply the rub, then place it fat-side up in the baking dish, on top of the sauerkraut.

6. Transfer the baking dish to the grill, close the lid, and roast the pork for 3 hours, or until a meat thermometer inserted in the thickest part of the meat reads 160ºF (71ºC).

7. Remove the pork roast from the baking dish and let rest for 5 minutes before slicing.

8. To serve, divide the sauerkraut-apple mixture among plates and top with the sliced pork.

Ham with Mustard

Prep time: 30 minutes | Cook time: 5 hours | Serves 12 to 15

1 (12- to 15-pound / 5.4- to 6.8-kg) whole bone-in ham, fully cooked
¼ cup yellow mustard
1 cup pineapple juice
½ cup packed light brown sugar
1 teaspoon ground cinnamon
½ teaspoon ground cloves

1. Supply your smoker with wood pellets and follow the manufacturer's specific start-up procedure. Preheat, with the lid closed, to 275ºF (135ºC).

2. Trim off the excess fat and skin from the ham, leaving a ¼-inch layer of fat. Put the ham in an aluminum foil–lined roasting pan.

3. On your kitchen stove top, in a medium saucepan over low heat, combine the mustard, pineapple juice, brown sugar, cinnamon, and cloves and simmer for 15 minutes, or until thick and reduced by about half.

4. Baste the ham with half of the pineapple-brown sugar syrup, reserving the rest for basting later in the cook.

5. Place the roasting pan on the grill, close the lid, and smoke for 4 hours.

6. Baste the ham with the remaining pineapple–brown sugar syrup and continue smoking with the lid closed for another hour, or until a meat thermometer inserted in the thickest part of the ham reads 140ºF (60ºC).

7. Remove the ham from the grill, tent with foil, and let rest for 20 minutes before carving.

Mustard Pork Ribs

Prep time: 15 minutes | Cook time: 6 hours | Serves 4

2 full slabs baby back ribs, back membranes removed

1 cup prepared table mustard

1 cup Paprika Dry Rub

1 cup apple juice, divided

1 cup packed light brown sugar, divided

1 cup Ketchup and BBQ Sauce, divided

1. Supply your smoker with wood pellets and follow the manufacturer's specific start-up procedure. Preheat, with the lid closed, to 150ºF (66ºC) to 180ºF (82ºC), or to the "Smoke" setting.

2. Coat the ribs with the mustard to help the rub stick and lock in moisture.

3. Generously apply the rub.

4. Place the ribs directly on the grill, close the lid, and smoke for 3 hours.

5. Increase the temperature to 225ºF (107ºC).

6. Remove the ribs from the grill and wrap each rack individually with aluminum foil, but before sealing tightly, add ½ cup apple juice and ½ cup brown sugar to each package.

7. Return the foil-wrapped ribs to the grill, close the lid, and smoke for 2 more hours.

8. Carefully unwrap the ribs and remove the foil completely. Coat each slab with ½ cup of barbecue sauce and continue smoking with the lid closed for 30 minutes to 1 hour, or until the meat tightens and has a reddish bark. For the perfect rack, the internal temperature should be 190ºF (88ºC).

Pork Cheese Nachos with Avocado

Prep time: 15 minutes | Cook time: 10 minutes | Serves 4

2 cups leftover smoked pulled pork

1 small sweet onion, diced

1 medium tomato, diced

1 jalapeño pepper, seeded and diced

1 garlic clove, minced

1 teaspoon salt

1 teaspoon freshly ground black pepper

1 bag tortilla chips

1 cup shredded Cheddar cheese

½ cup Ketchup and BBQ Sauce, divided

½ cup shredded jalapeño Monterey Jack cheese

Juice of ½ lime

1 avocado, halved, pitted, and sliced

2 tablespoons sour cream

1 tablespoon chopped fresh cilantro

1. Supply your smoker with wood pellets and follow the manufacturer's specific start-up procedure. Preheat, with the lid closed, to 375ºF (191ºC).

2. Heat the pulled pork in the microwave.

3. In a medium bowl, combine the onion, tomato, jalapeño, garlic, salt, and pepper, and set aside.

4. Arrange half of the tortilla chips in a large cast iron skillet. Spread half of the warmed pork on top and cover with the Cheddar cheese. Top with half of the onion-jalapeño mixture, then drizzle with ¼ cup of barbecue sauce.

5. Layer on the remaining tortilla chips, then the remaining pork and the Monterey Jack cheese. Top with the remaining onion-jalapeño mixture and drizzle with the remaining ¼ cup of barbecue sauce.

6. Place the skillet on the grill, close the lid, and smoke for about 10 minutes, or until the cheese is melted and bubbly. (Watch to make sure your chips don't burn!)

7. Squeeze the lime juice over the nachos, top with the avocado slices and sour cream, and garnish with the cilantro before serving hot.

Cream Cheese Pork Grits

Prep time: 20 minutes | Cook time: 30 to 40 minutes | Serves 8

2 cups chicken stock

1 cup water

1 cup quick-cooking grits

3 tablespoons unsalted butter

2 tablespoons minced garlic

1 medium onion, chopped

1 jalapeño pepper, stemmed, seeded, and chopped

1 teaspoon cayenne pepper

2 teaspoons red pepper flakes

1 tablespoon hot sauce

1 cup shredded Monterey Jack cheese

1 cup sour cream

Salt and freshly ground black pepper, to taste

2 eggs, beaten

⅓ cup half-and-half

3 cups leftover pulled pork (preferably smoked)

1. Supply your smoker with wood pellets and follow the manufacturer's specific start-up procedure. Preheat, with the lid closed, to 350ºF (177ºC).

2. On your kitchen stove top, in a large saucepan over high heat, bring the chicken stock and water to a boil.

3. Add the grits and reduce the heat to low, then stir in the butter, garlic, onion, jalapeño, cayenne, red pepper flakes, hot sauce, cheese, and sour cream. Season with salt and pepper, then cook for about 5 minutes.

4. Temper the beaten eggs and incorporate into the grits. Remove the saucepan from the heat and stir in the half-and-half and pulled pork.

5. Pour the grits into a greased grill-safe 9-by-13-inch casserole dish or aluminum pan.

6. Transfer to the grill, close the lid, and bake for 30 to 40 minutes, covering with aluminum foil toward the end of cooking if the grits start to get too brown on top.

Spareribs with BBQ Sauce

Prep time: 10 minutes | Cook time: 6 hours | Serves 4 to 5

2 racks pork spareribs, membrane removed from back

2 tablespoons yellow mustard

2 tablespoons chicken bouillon granules

1 tablespoon red pepper flakes

¼ cup apple juice, divided

1 cup Blueberry BBQ Sauce, plus more for serving

1. Supply your smoker with wood pellets and follow the manufacturer's specific start-up procedure. Preheat, with the lid closed, to 250ºF (121ºC).

2. Coat the ribs with the mustard, then sprinkle the ribs on all sides with the bouillon granules and red pepper flakes.

3. Place the ribs directly on the grill, close the lid, and smoke for 3 hours.

4. Remove the ribs from the grill and wrap each rack individually with aluminum foil, but before sealing tightly, add 2 tablespoons of apple juice to each package.

5. Place the foil-wrapped ribs back on the grill, close the lid, and continue smoking for 2 hours.

6. Carefully unwrap the ribs and remove the foil completely. Baste the ribs with the barbecue sauce, then smoke with the lid closed for 1 hour more.

7. Let the ribs rest for about 5 minutes before serving with additional barbecue sauce.

Cheese and Sausage Balls

Prep time: 15 minutes | Cook time: 30 minutes | Serves 4 to 5

1 pound (454 g) ground hot sausage, uncooked

8 ounces (227 g) cream cheese, softened

1 package mini filo dough shells

1. Supply your smoker with wood pellets and follow the manufacturer's specific start-up procedure. Preheat, with the lid closed, to 350ºF (177ºC).

2. In a large bowl, using your hands, thoroughly mix together the sausage and cream cheese until well blended.

3. Place the filo dough shells on a rimmed perforated pizza pan or into a mini muffin tin.

4. Roll the sausage and cheese mixture into 1-inch balls and place into the filo shells.

5. Place the pizza pan or mini muffin tin on the grill, close the lid, and smoke the sausage balls for 30 minutes, or until cooked through and the sausage is no longer pink.

6. Plate and serve warm.

Mustard Pork Shoulder

Prep time: 30 minutes | Cook time: 8 to 9 hours | Serves 10

1 (5-pound / 2.3-kg) Boston butt (pork shoulder)

¼ cup prepared table mustard

½ cup Paprika Dry Rub or your favorite rub, divided

2 cups apple juice

½ cup salt

Ketchup and BBQ Sauce, for serving

1. Slather the meat with the mustard and coat with ¼ cup of the dry rub.

2. In a spray bottle, mix together the apple juice and salt and shake until the salt is dissolved.

3. Supply your smoker with wood pellets and follow the manufacturer's specific start-up procedure. Preheat, with the lid closed, to 225ºF (107ºC).

4. Place the pork fat-side up in an aluminum pan, transfer to the grill, close the lid, and smoke

for 8 to 9 hours, spritzing well all over with the salted apple juice every hour, until a meat thermometer inserted in the thickest part of the meat reads 205ºF (96ºC). Cover the pork loosely with aluminum foil toward the end of cooking, if necessary, to keep the top from blackening.

5. Drain the liquid from the pan, cover, and allow the meat to cool for a few minutes before using two forks to shred it.

6. Sprinkle the remaining rub over the meat and serve with barbecue sauce.

Beer Brats Rolls

Prep time: 10 minutes | Cook time: 2 hours | Serves 10

4 (12-ounce / 340-g) cans beer

2 onions, sliced into rings

2 green bell peppers, sliced into rings

2 tablespoons unsalted butter, plus more for the rolls

2 tablespoons red pepper flakes

10 brats, uncooked

10 hoagie rolls, split

Mustard, for serving

1. On your kitchen stove top, in a large saucepan over high heat, bring the beer, onions, peppers, butter, and red pepper flakes to a boil.

2. Supply your smoker with wood pellets and follow the manufacturer's specific start-up procedure. Preheat, with the lid closed, to 225ºF (107ºC).

3. Place a disposable pan on one side of grill, and pour the warmed beer mixture into it, creating a "brat tub".

4. Place the brats on the other side of the grill, directly on the grate, and close the lid and smoke for 1 hour, turning 2 or 3 times.

5. Add the brats to the pan with the onions and peppers, cover tightly with aluminum foil, and continue smoking with the lid closed for 30 minutes to 1 hour, or until a meat thermometer inserted in the brats reads 160ºF (71ºC).

6. Butter the cut sides of the hoagie rolls and toast cut-side down on the grill.

7. Using a slotted spoon, remove the brats, onions, and peppers from the cooking liquid and discard the liquid.

8. Serve the brats on the toasted buns, topped with the onions and peppers and mustard.

Pork Tenderloins

Prep time: 20 minutes | Cook time: 1½ hours | Serves 8 to 12

2 (1½ to 2-pound / 680- to 907-g) pork tenderloins

¼ cup roasted garlic–flavored extra-virgin olive oil

¼ cup Sweet Dry Rub with Paprika or Pork Dry Rub

1. Trim any excess fat and silver skin from the meat.

2. Rub all sides of the tenderloins with the olive oil and dust with the rub.

3. Wrap the seasoned tenderloins in plastic wrap and refrigerate for 2 to 4 hours.

4. Configure your wood pellet smoker-grill for indirect cooking and preheat to 230ºF (110ºC) using hickory or apple pellets.

5. Remove the plastic wrap from the meat and insert your wood pellet smoker-grill probes or a remote meat probe into the thickest part of each tenderloin. If your grill does not have meat probe capabilities or you don't own a remote meat probe then use an instant-read digital

thermometer during the cook for internal temperature readings.

6. Place the tenderloins directly on the grill and smoke them for 45 minutes at 230ºF (110ºC).

7. Increase the pit temperature to 350ºF (177ºC) and finish cooking the tenderloins for about 45 more minutes, until the internal temperature at the thickest part reaches 145ºF (63ºC).

8. Rest the pork tenderloins under a loose foil tent for 10 minutes before serving.

Smoked Ham

Prep time: 15 minutes | Cook time: 2½ to 3 hours | Serves 8 to 12

1 (10-pound / 4.5-kg) applewood-smoked, boneless, fully cooked, ready-to-eat ham or bone-in smoked ham

1. Remove the ham from its packaging and let sit at room temperature for 30 minutes.

2. Configure your wood pellet smoker-grill for indirect cooking and preheat to 180ºF (82ºC) using apple or hickory pellets depending on what type of wood was used for the initial smoking.

3. Place the ham directly on the grill grates and smoke the ham for 1 hour at 180ºF (82ºC).

4. After an hour, increase pit temperature to 350ºF (177ºC).

5. Cook the ham until the internal temperature reaches 140ºF (60ºC), about 1½ to 2 more hours.

6. Remove the ham and wrap in foil for 15 minutes before carving against the grain.

Pork Ribs with Paprika

Prep time: 30 minutes | Cook time: 3 to 3½ hours | Serves 6

1 (5-pound / 2.3-kg) rack of pork, about 6 ribs

¼ cup roasted garlic–flavored extra-virgin olive oil

6 tablespoons Sweet Dry Rub with Paprika, Pork Dry Rub, or your favorite pork roast rub

1. Trim off the fat cap and silver skin from the rack of pork. Just like a slab of ribs, a rack of pork has a membrane on the bones. Remove the membrane from the bones by working a spoon handle under the bone membrane until you can grab the membrane with a paper towel to pull it off.

2. Rub the olive oil liberally on all sides of the meat. Season with the rub, covering all sides of the meat.

3. Double wrap the seasoned rack of pork in plastic wrap and refrigerate for 2 to 4 hours or overnight.

4. Remove the seasoned rack of pork from the refrigerator and let sit at room temperature for 30 minutes before cooking.

5. Configure your wood pellet smoker-grill for indirect cooking and preheat to 225ºF (107ºC) using hickory pellets.

6. Insert your wood pellet smoker-grill meat probe or a remote meat probe into the thickest part of the rack of pork. If your grill does not have meat probe capabilities or you don't own a remote meat probe then, use an instant-read digital thermometer during the cook for internal temperature readings.

7. Place the rack rib-side down directly on the grill grates.

8. Smoke the rack of pork for 3 to 3½ hours, until the internal temperature reaches 140ºF (60ºC).

9. Remove from the meat from the smoker, and let it rest under a loose foil tent for 15 minutes before carving.

Spinach and Pork with Bacon

Prep time: 30 minutes | Cook time: 1 hour | Serves 6 to 8

1 (3-pound / 1.4-kg) boneless ribeye pork loin roast

4 tablespoons extra-virgin olive oil, divided

2 tablespoons Pork Dry Rub or your favorite pork seasoning

4 bacon slices

6 cups fresh spinach

1 small red onion, diced

6 cloves garlic, cut into thin slivers

¾ cup shredded Mozzarella cheese

1.   Trim away any excess fat and silver skin.

2.   Butterfly the pork loin or ask your butcher to butterfly it for you. There are many excellent videos online with detailed instructions on the different techniques for butterflying a loin roast.

3.   Rub 2 tablespoons of the olive oil on each side of the butterflied roast, and season both sides with the rub.

4.   Cook the bacon in a large skillet over medium heat. Crumble and set aside. Reserve the bacon fat.

5.   In a large skillet over medium-high heat, heat 2 tablespoons of the reserved bacon fat, wilt the spinach, and set aside.

6.   Using the same large skillet over medium-high heat, heat 2 additional tablespoons of bacon fat and cook the onion until it is translucent, about 8 minutes.

7.   Layer the wilted spinach, garlic slivers, shredded Mozzarella, crumbled bacon, and onion in the center of the butterflied pork loin.

8.   Roll the butterflied pork loin tightly. Tie off the stuffed ribeye pork loin with butcher's twine at 2-inch intervals.

9.   Configure your wood pellet smoker-grill for indirect cooking and preheat to 375ºF (191ºC) using any pellets.

10.   Insert your wood pellet smoker-grill meat probe or a remote meat probe into the thickest part of the pork loin. If your grill does not have meat probe capabilities or you don't own a remote meat probe, then use an instant-read digital thermometer during the cook for internal temperature readings.

11.   Grill the pork loin for 60 to 75 minutes, or until the internal temperature at the thickest part reaches 140ºF (60ºC).

12.   Rest the pork loin under a loose foil tent for 15 minutes before carving against the grain.

Pork Rib Racks

Prep time: 30 minutes | Cook time: 5 to 6 hours | Serves 6 to 8

3 St. Louis-style pork rib racks

1 cup plus 1 tablespoon Sweet Dry Rub with Paprika or your favorite pork rub

1.   Remove the membrane on the underside of the rib racks by inserting a spoon handle between the membrane and rib bones. Grab the membrane with a paper towel and slowly pull it down the rack to remove.

2.   Rub both sides of the ribs with a liberal amount of the rub.

3.   Configure your wood pellet smoker-grill for indirect cooking and preheat to 225ºF (107ºC) using hickory or apple pellets.

4.   If using a rib rack, place the ribs in the rack on the grill grates. Otherwise you can use Teflon-coated fiberglass mats, or place the ribs directly on the grill grates.

5.   Smoke the ribs at 225ºF (107ºC) for 5 to 6 hours with hickory pellets until the internal

temperature, at the thickest part of the ribs, reaches 185ºF (85ºC) to 190ºF (88ºC).

6.   Rest the ribs under a loose foil tent for 10 minutes before carving and serving.

Bacon Cheese Stuffed Jalapeños

Prep time: 10 minutes | Cook time: 1 hour | Serves 24 jalapeño poppers

12 jalapeños, 3 to 4 inches in size
1 (8-ounce / 227-g) package cream cheese, softened
1 cup shredded cheese (Cheddar, Monterey Jack, Pepper Jack or taco blend)
¼ cup sugar-forward rub (such as Meat Church Honey Hog BBQ Rub)
12 slices bacon

1.   Prepare your Traeger by turning it to the SMOKE setting. Wait about 5 minutes for it to produce smoke, then set the Traeger to run at 275ºF (135ºC).

2.   Slice the tops off the jalapeños as close to the stem as possible. Slice the jalapeño vertically and using your (gloved) finger or a small spoon, scoop out all the ribs and seeds and discard them.

3.   In a bowl, mix the cream cheese, shredded cheese and rub until combined.

4.   Slice the bacon in half vertically to make 24 pieces.

5.   Spoon (or pipe, using a food storage bag) the cheese mixture into the jalapeños, then wrap each with a piece of bacon. Place the jalapeños on a sheet tray and put the tray on the smoker for 30 minutes.

6.   Increase the temperature of the smoker to 375ºF (191ºC) and smoke another 30 minutes to crisp the bacon.

Bacon Sausage Cheese Fatty

Prep time: 15 minutes | Cook time: 2 hours | Serves 6

1 pound (454 g) bacon
2 to 3 tablespoons pork rub
1 tablespoon olive oil
1 medium onion (white, yellow, Spanish or sweet), peeled and sliced into ¼-inch strips
1 medium green pepper, stemmed, seeded and cut into ¼-inch strips
1 medium red pepper, stemmed, seeded and cut into ¼-inch strips
½ teaspoon salt
½ teaspoon black pepper
2 pounds (907 g) ground sausage (your choice of hot, sweet or breakfast; without casing)
¼ cup grated Parmesan cheese
Your favorite BBQ sauce, for serving

1.   To create a bacon weave, lay eight slices of bacon vertically very close together on plastic wrap. The bacon slices should all be facing the same direction (fat side facing one way, meat side facing the other). Working with one strip at a time, arrange eight additional strips perpendicular to the first ones, weaving the strips over and under to form a lattice. Make sure your weave is as tight as possible when finished.

2.   Sprinkle approximately 2 tablespoons of the rub on the weave, adding more as necessary. You want your bacon weave to be well coated but not overly dredged. You should have a nice even covering of rub on the weave.

3.   Heat the oil in a large skillet over medium-high heat. Add the onion, peppers, salt and pepper, and cook about 5 minutes, or until soft. Allow the mixture to cool, then strain off excess water using a colander.

4. Layer the sausage directly on top of the bacon weave, patting down gently and keeping the same thickness throughout the layer (so it will cook evenly). Next, spoon the pepper mixture evenly on top of the sausage and sprinkle with Parmesan cheese. Carefully separate the front edge of the sausage layer from the bacon weave and begin rolling into a log. You want to include all layers except the bacon weave. Try to seal any holes and pinch off the ends. The sausage should now be in the shape of a log. Next, roll the sausage forward, wrapping it in the bacon weave. The bacon seam should be underneath the roll when you are done. Sprinkle more rub on the outside of the roll.

5. Meanwhile, prepare your Traeger by turning it to the SMOKE setting. Wait about 5 minutes for it to produce smoke, then set the Traeger to run at 250ºF (121ºC).

6. Place the sausage roll directly on the smoker grates and close the lid. Allow the roll to cook for about 2 hours, or until an instant-read thermometer inserted into the center of the roll reads 165ºF (74ºC).

7. Remove the roll from the smoker and allow it to cool for 5 minutes. Using a sharp knife, slice the roll into ½-inch-thick pieces. Drizzle with BBQ sauce before serving.

Blueberry Bacon Sausage Fatty

Prep time: 10 minutes | Cook time: 2 hours | Serves 6

1 pound (454 g) bacon
1 (16-ounce / 454-g) roll ground breakfast sausage (such as Jimmy Dean)
2 tablespoons pork rub
4 large store-bought blueberry muffins, preferably with sugar topping
6 slices pound cake, for serving (optional)
½ cup pure maple syrup, for serving

1. Create a bacon weave on plastic wrap. Make sure your weave is as tight as possible when finished.

2. Layer the sausage directly on top of the bacon weave, patting down gently and keeping the same thickness throughout the layer (so it will cook evenly). Sprinkle the rub evenly over the sausage to coat. Next, using only the tops of the muffins, crumble the blueberry muffins with your hands onto the sausage. Make sure to cover the sausage with the muffins as evenly as possible.

3. Carefully separate the front edge of the sausage layer from the bacon weave and begin rolling into a log. You want to include all layers except the bacon weave. Try to seal any holes and pinch off the ends. The sausage should now be in the shape of a log. Next, roll the sausage forward, wrapping it in the bacon weave. The bacon seam should be underneath the roll when you are done.

4. Meanwhile, prepare your Traeger by turning it to the SMOKE setting. Wait about 5 minutes for it to produce smoke, then set the Traeger to run at 250ºF (121ºC).

5. Place your sausage roll directly on the smoker grates and close the lid. Allow the roll to cook for about 2 hours, or until an instant-read thermometer inserted into the center of the roll reads 165ºF (74ºC). Remove the roll from the smoker and allow it to cool for 5 minutes.

6. If serving this dish on pound cake, slice the cake into ¾-inch slices and put directly on the smoker grate with the lid open, turning once to toast both sides. Using a sharp knife, slice the roll into ½-inch-thick pieces. Drizzle with maple syrup before serving.

Pork Belly with Bourbon

Prep time: 10 minutes | Cook time: 5 hours | Serves 10 to 12

3 pounds (1.4 kg) pork belly

1 tablespoon mustard powder

1 teaspoon cumin

¾ teaspoon freshly ground black pepper

1½ tablespoons kosher salt

¼ cup maple syrup

2 tablespoons honey bourbon (such as Jack Honey)

1. Rinse and dry the pork belly. Remove the hard outer skin if present, cutting close to the edge of the fat to leave as much fat on the meat as possible.

2. Combine the mustard powder, cumin, black pepper and salt in a small bowl. Rub half of the mixture on the pork belly on all sides.

3. In a plastic resealable freezer bag, combine the maple syrup, bourbon and the remainder of the dry spice mixture. Place the pork belly in the plastic bag and massage to coat. Seal the bag, making sure to squeeze out excess air. Place the bag in the refrigerator; turn the bag over occasionally to ensure all ingredients coat the meat evenly. Refrigerate for at least 24 hours and up to 3 days.

4. When ready to cook, prepare your Traeger by turning it to the SMOKE setting. Wait about 5 minutes for it to produce smoke, then set the Traeger to run at 225ºF (107ºC).

5. Remove the pork belly from the brine and put it in a disposable aluminum pan, fat-side up. When the grill has reached the correct temperature, place the pan inside the smoker directly on the grates and close the door. Let the pork belly cook about 5 hours, or until the internal temperature reaches 175ºF (79ºC).

6. Remove the pork belly from the smoker and allow it to cool for about 5 minutes. Slice or cube and enjoy!

Honey Pork with Garlic

Prep time: 10 minutes | Cook time: 2½ to 3 hours | Serves 4

1 2-inch piece fresh ginger

4 large cloves garlic

¾ cup soy sauce

½ cup honey

1 tablespoon rice wine or white vinegar

1 tablespoon olive oil

½ teaspoon black pepper

½ teaspoon ground chile

2 tablespoons cornstarch

1½ pounds (680 g) pork tenderloin, silver skin removed if attached

1. Peel the ginger and chop it coarsely. Lay the ginger on a cutting board and smash the ginger to release its aromas and flavors by taking the back of a chef knife and pressing it firmly onto the ginger. Do the same for the four cloves of garlic.

2. In a small pot over medium heat, add the soy sauce, honey, garlic, ginger, vinegar, olive oil, black pepper and ground chile. Stir until simmering, then add the cornstarch, stirring constantly. Remove from the heat when the mixture starts to boil. The sauce should be smooth and thicker than when you started.

3. Meanwhile, prepare your Traeger to run at 225ºF (107ºC).

4. Place the tenderloin in a disposable aluminum tray and pour the sauce over the tenderloin. Put the tray in the smoker and cook for 2½ to 3 hours or until the internal temperature reaches 145ºF (63ºC). Let the tenderloin rest for 5 minutes before slicing.

Pork with Blackberry

Prep time: 10 minutes | Cook time: 12 to 16 minutes | Serves 6

2 (1- to 1½-pound / 454- to 680-g) pork tenderloins
2 tablespoons olive oil
2 teaspoons kosher salt
1 teaspoon freshly ground black pepper
2 teaspoons garlic powder
2 teaspoons onion powder
Pinch of cayenne pepper
¾ cup blackberry preserves (seedless)

1. Prepare your Traeger to run at 400°F (204°C).

2. Trim and clean the pork tenderloins of excess fat and silver skin. Coat each with the olive oil and season with the salt, black pepper, garlic powder, onion powder and cayenne pepper. Mix the blackberry preserves well with a fork, for easier spreading. Place the tenderloins on the preheated grate of the Traeger and generously brush all visible sides of the pork tenderloins with the blackberry preserves.

3. Leave the lid open and cook for 3 to 4 minutes, turn over and coat the other side with blackberry preserves. Turn over and brush on preserves twice more, cooking for 3 to 4 minutes each time, until an internal temperature of 145°F (63°C) is reached. Remove the tenderloins from the grill and allow the meat to rest for at least 10 minutes before slicing.

CHAPTER 4: BEEF

Breaded Bacon Cheese Beef Meatloaf

Prep time: 15 minutes | Cook time: 2 hours | Serves 8 to 10

1 tablespoon canola oil

2 garlic cloves, finely chopped

1 medium onion, finely chopped

1 poblano chile, stemmed, seeded, and finely chopped

2 pounds (907 g) extra-lean ground beef

2 tablespoons Montreal steak seasoning

1 tablespoon A.1. Steak Sauce

½ pound (227 g) bacon, cooked and crumbled

2 cups shredded Swiss cheese

1 egg, beaten

2 cups breadcrumbs

½ cup Tiger Sauce

1. On your stove top, heat the canola oil in a medium sauté pan over medium-high heat. Add the garlic, onion, and poblano, and sauté for 3 to 5 minutes, or until the onion is just barely translucent.

2. Supply your smoker with wood pellets and follow the manufacturer's specific start-up procedure. Preheat, with the lid closed, to 225ºF (107ºC).

3. In a large bowl, combine the sautéed vegetables, ground beef, steak seasoning, steak sauce, bacon, Swiss cheese, egg, and breadcrumbs. Mix with your hands until well incorporated, then shape into a loaf.

4. Put the meatloaf in a cast iron skillet and place it on the grill. Close the lid and smoke for 2 hours, or until a meat thermometer inserted in the loaf reads 165ºF (74ºC).

5. Top with the meatloaf with the Tiger Sauce, remove from the grill, and let rest for about 10 minutes before serving.

Glazed London Broil

Prep time: 20 minutes | Cook time: 12 to 16 minutes | Serves 3 to 4

1 (1½- to 2-pound / 680- to 907-g) London broil or top round steak

¼ cup soy sauce

2 tablespoons white wine

2 tablespoons extra-virgin olive oil

¼ cup chopped scallions

2 tablespoons packed brown sugar

2 garlic cloves, minced

2 teaspoons red pepper flakes

1 teaspoon freshly ground black pepper

1. Using a meat mallet, pound the steak lightly all over on both sides to break down its fibers and tenderize. You are not trying to pound down the thickness.

2. In a medium bowl, make the marinade by combining the soy sauce, white wine, olive oil, scallions, brown sugar, garlic, red pepper flakes, and black pepper.

3. Put the steak in a shallow plastic container with a lid and pour the marinade over the meat. Cover and refrigerate for 4 hours.

4. Remove the steak from the marinade, shaking off any excess, and discard the marinade.

5. Supply your smoker with wood pellets and follow the manufacturer's specific start-up procedure. Preheat, with the lid closed, to 350ºF (177ºC).

6. Place the steak directly on the grill, close the lid, and smoke for 6 minutes. Flip, then smoke

with the lid closed for 6 to 10 minutes more, or until a meat thermometer inserted in the meat reads 130ºF (54ºC) for medium-rare.

7. Let the steak rest for about 10 minutes before slicing and serving. The meat's temperature will rise by about 5 degrees while it rests.

Beef Cheese Burgers

Prep time: 35 minutes | Cook time: 20 to 25 minutes | Serves 4

1 pound (454 g) lean ground beef

1 tablespoon minced garlic

1 teaspoon Better Than Bouillon Beef Base

1 teaspoon dried chives

1 teaspoon freshly ground black pepper

8 slices Gruyère cheese, divided

½ cup soy sauce

1 tablespoon extra-virgin olive oil

1 teaspoon liquid smoke

3 medium onions, cut into thick slices (do not separate the rings)

1 loaf French bread, cut into 8 slices

4 slices provolone cheese

1. In a large bowl, mix together the ground beef, minced garlic, beef base, chives, and pepper until well blended.

2. Divide the meat mixture and shape into 8 thin burger patties.

3. Top each of 4 patties with one slice of Gruyère, then top with the remaining 4 patties to create 4 stuffed burgers.

4. Supply your smoker with wood pellets and follow the manufacturer's specific start-up procedure. Preheat, with the lid closed, to 425ºF (218ºC).

5. Arrange the burgers directly on one side of the grill, close the lid, and smoke for 10 minutes.

Flip and smoke with the lid closed for 10 to 15 minutes more, or until a meat thermometer inserted in the burgers reads 160ºF (71ºC). Add another Gruyère slice to the burgers during the last 5 minutes of smoking to melt.

6. Meanwhile, in a small bowl, combine the soy sauce, olive oil, and liquid smoke.

7. Arrange the onion slices on the grill and baste on both sides with the soy sauce mixture. Smoke with the lid closed for 20 minutes, flipping halfway through.

8. Lightly toast the French bread slices on the grill. Layer each of 4 slices with a burger patty, a slice of provolone cheese, and some of the smoked onions. Top each with another slice of toasted French bread. Serve immediately.

Beef Shoulder Clod with Pepper

Prep time: 10 minutes | Cook time: 12 to 16 hours | Serves 16 to 20

½ cup sea salt

½ cup freshly ground black pepper

1 tablespoon red pepper flakes

1 tablespoon minced garlic

1 tablespoon cayenne pepper

1 tablespoon smoked paprika

1 (13- to 15-pound / 5.9- to 6.8-kg) beef shoulder clod

1. In a small bowl, combine the salt, pepper, red pepper flakes, minced garlic, cayenne pepper, and smoked paprika to create a rub. Generously apply it to the beef shoulder.

2. Supply your smoker with wood pellets and follow the manufacturer's specific start-up procedure. Preheat, with the lid closed, to 250ºF (121ºC).

3. Put the meat on the grill grate, close the lid, and smoke for 12 to 16 hours, or until a meat

thermometer inserted deeply into the beef reads 195ºF (91ºC). You may need to cover the clod with aluminum foil toward the end of smoking to prevent over-browning.

4.   Let the meat rest for about 15 minutes before slicing against the grain and serving.

Corned Beef and Cabbage

Prep time: 30 minutes | Cook time: 4 to 5 hours | Serves 6 to 8

Corned Beef:

1 gallon water

1 (3- to 4-pound / 1.4- to 1.8-kg) point cut corned beef brisket with pickling spice packet

1 tablespoon freshly ground black pepper

1 tablespoon garlic powder

½ cup molasses

1 teaspoon ground mustard

Cabbage:

1 head green cabbage

4 tablespoons (½ stick) butter

2 tablespoons rendered bacon fat

1 chicken bouillon cube, crushed

Make the Corned Beef

1.   In a large container with a lid, combine the water and the corned beef pickling spice packet and submerge the corned beef in it. Cover and refrigerate overnight, changing the water as often as you remember to do so—ideally, every 3 hours while you're awake—to soak out some of the curing salt originally added.

2.   Supply your smoker with wood pellets and follow the manufacturer's specific start-up procedure. Preheat, with the lid closed, to 275ºF (135ºC).

3.   Remove the meat from the brining liquid, pat it dry, and generously rub with the black pepper and garlic powder.

4.   Put the seasoned corned beef directly on the grill, fat-side up, close the lid, and grill for 2 hours. Remove from the grill when done.

5.   In a small bowl, combine the molasses and ground mustard and pour half of this mixture into the bottom of a disposable aluminum pan.

6.   Transfer the meat to the pan, fat-side up, and pour the remaining molasses mixture on top, spreading it evenly over the meat. Cover tightly with aluminum foil.

7.   Transfer the pan to the grill, close the lid, and continue smoking the corned beef for 2 to 3 hours, or until a meat thermometer inserted in the thickest part reads 185ºF (85ºC).

Make the Cabbage

8.   While the brisket is smoking, core the cabbage and fill the resulting cavity with the butter, rendered bacon fat, and crushed chicken bouillon cube.

9.   Wrap the cabbage in foil about two-thirds of the way up the sides to protect the outer leaves, but do not completely cover, and place on the grill alongside the corned beef about an hour before the meat is expected to be finished.

10. Remove both the corned beef and the cabbage from the grill. Let the meat rest for 15 minutes, then slice against the grain.

11. Carefully unwrap the cabbage and pour the compound butter from the cavity into a large casserole dish.

12. Chop the cabbage and add to the casserole dish, then top with the sliced corned beef to serve.

Beef Cheeseburger Pies

Prep time: 35 minutes | Cook time: 10 minutes | Makes 6

½ pound (227 g) lean ground beef

1 tablespoon minced onion

1 tablespoon steak seasoning

1 cup shredded Monterey Jack and Colby cheese blend

8 slices white American cheese, divided

2 (14-ounce / 397-g) refrigerated prepared pizza dough sheets, divided

2 eggs, beaten with 2 tablespoons water (egg wash), divided

24 hamburger dill pickle chips

2 tablespoons sesame seeds

6 slices tomato, for garnish

Ketchup and mustard, for serving

1. Supply your smoker with wood pellets and follow the manufacturer's specific start-up procedure. Preheat, with the lid closed, to 325ºF (163ºC).

2. On your stove top, in a medium sauté pan over medium-high heat, brown the ground beef for 4 to 5 minutes, or until cooked through. Add the minced onion and steak seasoning.

3. Toss in the shredded cheese blend and 2 slices of American cheese, and stir until melted and fully incorporated.

4. Remove the cheeseburger mixture from the heat and set aside.

5. Make sure the dough is well chilled for easier handling. Working quickly, roll out one prepared pizza crust on parchment paper and brush with half of the egg wash.

6. Arrange the remaining 6 slices of American cheese on the dough to outline 6 hand pies.

7. Top each cheese slice with ¼ cup of the cheeseburger mixture, spreading slightly inside the imaginary lines of the hand pies.

8. Place 4 pickle slices on top of the filling for each pie.

9. Top the whole thing with the other prepared pizza crust and cut between the cheese slices to create 6 hand pies.

10. Using kitchen scissors, cut the parchment to further separate the pies, but leave them on the paper.

11. Using a fork dipped in egg wash, seal the edges of the pies on all sides. Baste the tops of the pies with the remaining egg wash and sprinkle with the sesame seeds.

12. Remove the pies from the parchment paper and gently place on the grill grate. Close the lid and smoke for 5 minutes, then carefully flip and smoke with the lid closed for 5 more minutes, or until browned.

13. Top with the sliced tomato and serve with ketchup and mustard.

Filet Mignons

Prep time: 10 minutes | Cook time: 12 to 14 minutes | Serves 2

2 (1¼-inch-thick) filet mignons

2 teaspoons sea salt

2 teaspoons freshly ground black pepper

2 teaspoons minced garlic

2 teaspoons onion powder

1. Supply your smoker with wood pellets and follow the manufacturer's specific start-up procedure. Preheat, with the lid closed, to 450ºF (232ºC).

2. In a small bowl, combine the salt, pepper, minced garlic, and onion powder to form a rub, and generously apply it to both sides of the steaks.

3. Lay the steaks on grill grate, close the lid, and smoke for 7 minutes. Flip and continue smoking with the lid closed for 5 to 7 minutes, or until the internal temperature reaches 125ºF (52ºC) to 130ºF (54ºC) for medium-rare. Remove the steaks from the grill.

4. Let the meat rest for 5 minutes before serving.

Beef Pastrami with Coriander

Prep time: 10 minutes | Cook time: 4 to 5 hours | Serves 12

1 gallon water, plus ½ cup

½ cup packed light brown sugar

1 (3- to 4-pound / 1.4- to 1.8-kg) point cut corned beef brisket with brine mix packet

2 tablespoons freshly ground black pepper

¼ cup ground coriander

1. In a large container with a lid, combine 1 gallon of water, the brown sugar, and the corned beef spice packet, then submerge the corned beef in it. Cover and refrigerate overnight, changing the water as often as you remember to do so—ideally, every 3 hours while you're awake—to soak out some of the curing salt originally added.

2. Supply your smoker with wood pellets and follow the manufacturer's specific start-up procedure. Preheat, with the lid closed, to 275ºF (135ºC).

3. In a small bowl, combine the black pepper and ground coriander to form a rub.

4. Drain the meat, pat it dry, and generously coat on all sides with the rub.

5. Place the corned beef directly on the grill, fat-side up, close the lid, and smoke for 3 hours to 3 hours 30 minutes, or until a meat thermometer inserted in the thickest part reads 175ºF (79ºC) to 185ºF (85ºC).

6. Pour the remaining ½ cup of water into the bottom of a disposable roasting pan. Add the corned beef, cover tightly with aluminum foil, and smoke on the grill with the lid closed for an additional 30 minutes to 1 hour.

7. Remove the meat from the grill and let cool for about 10 minutes. Transfer to a plate and refrigerate for at least 1 hour before thinly slicing and serving.

Rump Roast

Prep time: 10 minutes | Cook time: 3 to 4 hours | Serves 6 to 8

1 (3- to 4-pound / 1.4- to 1.8-kg) rump roast

Extra-virgin olive oil, for rubbing

2 tablespoons steak seasoning

1 tablespoon minced garlic

1. Supply your smoker with wood pellets and follow the manufacturer's specific start-up procedure. Preheat, with the lid closed, to 425ºF (218ºC).

2. Rub the roast with olive oil and generously apply steak seasoning and minced garlic.

3. Put the meat directly on the grill and sear all surfaces of the roast for 2 to 5 minutes per side. Remove from the grill.

4. Reduce the temperature to 225ºF (107ºC).

5. Place the roast back on the grill, close the lid, and smoke for 3 to 4 hours, or until a meat thermometer inserted in the thickest part of the roast reads 120ºF (49ºC) to 155ºF (68ºC), based on your desired doneness.

6. Remove the roast from the grill, tent with aluminum foil, and let rest for about 10 minutes before slicing against the grain to serve.

Chuck Roast with BBQ Sauce

Prep time: 15 minutes | Cook time: 8 hours | Serves 6

1 (3-pound / 1.4-kg) chuck roast

3 tablespoons Paprika Dry Rub

¾ cup Ketchup and BBQ Sauce, divided

1. Supply your smoker with wood pellets and follow the manufacturer's specific start-up procedure. Preheat, with the lid closed, to 275ºF (135ºC).

2. Liberally season the chuck roast with the dry rub.

3. Place the meat directly on the grill, close the lid, and smoke for about 5 hours, or until you see a dark bark on the surface of the meat and a meat thermometer inserted in the thickest part reads 165ºF (74ºC).

4. Wrap the meat tightly in aluminum foil and continue smoking with the lid closed for about another hour, or until the internal temperature registers 195ºF (91ºC) on the meat thermometer.

5. Remove from the heat and let rest for 15 to 20 minutes before cutting into 2-inch cubes.

6. Transfer the cubes to a disposable baking pan and toss with ½ cup of barbecue sauce.

7. Place the pan on the grill, close the lid, and smoke for another 1 hour 30 minutes to 2 hours, or until hot and bubbly, adding the remaining ¼ cup of barbecue sauce in the last 30 minutes of cooking.

8. Serve immediately.

Prime Rib with Chimichurri Sauce

Prep time: 15 minutes | Cook time: 1 hour | Serves 6 to 8

1 (3- to 4-pound / 1.4- to 1.8-kg) prime rib

Butcher's string

1 tablespoon coarse salt

1 tablespoon freshly ground black pepper

1 tablespoon garlic powder

Chimichurri Sauce, for serving

1. Let the roast sit at room temperature for about 1 hour, then tie with butcher's string in several places to hold it together during the smoking process.

2. Supply your smoker with wood pellets and follow the manufacturer's specific start-up procedure. Preheat, with the lid closed, to 450ºF (232ºC).

3. In a small bowl, combine the salt, pepper, and garlic powder, and rub this mixture all over the prime rib.

4. Place the meat bone-side down in a roasting pan with a rack and put the pan on the grill.

5. Close the lid and smoke the prime rib for 30 minutes, then reduce the heat to 300ºF (149ºC).

6. Continue to roast the meat with the lid closed for 25 to 50 minutes, depending on the size and desired internal temperature. Total cook time will be about 20 minutes per pound, but do not remove from the heat before a meat thermometer inserted deep into the middle of the meat reads between 120ºF (49ºC) (rare) and 155ºF (68ºC) (well-done).

7. Let the prime rib rest for 10 to 20 minutes before removing the string and removing the bones.

8. Slice the steak, transfer to plates, and serve drizzled with chimichurri sauce.

Steaks with Cheese Butter

Prep time: 10 minutes | Cook time: 45 to 50 minutes | Serves 4

4 tablespoons (½ stick) unsalted butter, at room temperature

½ cup blue cheese crumbles

4 (14-ounce / 397-g) T-bone steaks, 1 inch thick

2 tablespoons kosher salt

1 tablespoon freshly ground black pepper

2 tablespoons minced garlic

1.   In a medium bowl, stir together the butter and blue cheese crumbles and set aside, but do not refrigerate unless making in advance.

2.   Supply your smoker with wood pellets and follow the manufacturer's specific start-up procedure. Preheat, with the lid closed, to 165ºF (74ºC).

3.   Season the steaks with the salt, pepper, and garlic.

4.   Arrange the steaks directly on the grill, close the lid, and smoke for 30 minutes.

5.   Increase the heat to 450ºF (232ºC) and smoke for an additional 15 minutes for medium-rare, or longer for desired doneness, turning once, until a meat thermometer inserted in the meat reads 120ºF (49ºC) to 155ºF (68ºC).

6.   Remove the steaks from the grill and let rest for 3 to 5 minutes before serving topped with the blue cheese butter.

Tri-Tip Bottom Sirloin

Prep time: 15 minutes | Cook time: 45 minutes to 1 hour | Serves 4 to 6

2 teaspoons sea salt

2 teaspoons freshly ground black pepper

2 teaspoons onion powder

2 teaspoons garlic powder

2 teaspoons dried oregano

1 teaspoon cayenne pepper

1 teaspoon ground sage

1 teaspoon finely chopped fresh rosemary

1 (1½ – to 2-pound / 680- to 907-g) tri-tip bottom sirloin

1.   Supply your smoker with wood pellets and follow the manufacturer's specific start-up procedure. Preheat, with the lid closed, to 425ºF (218ºC).

2.   In a small bowl, combine the salt, pepper, onion powder, garlic powder, oregano, cayenne pepper, sage, and rosemary to create a rub.

3.   Season the meat all over with the rub and lay it directly on the grill.

4.   Close the lid and smoke for 45 minutes to 1 hour, or until a meat thermometer inserted in the thickest part of the meat reads 120ºF (49ºC) for rare, 130ºF (54ºC) for medium-rare, or 140ºF (60ºC) for medium, keeping in mind that the meat will come up in temperature by about another 5ºF during the rest period.

5.   Remove the tri-tip from the heat, tent with aluminum foil, and let rest for 15 minutes before slicing against the grain.

Beef Sausage Cheese Stuffed Peppers

Prep time: 30 minutes | Cook time: 1 hour 15 minutes | Serves 4

4 large bell peppers, tops removed, cored, and seeded

½ pound (227 g) ground beef

½ pound (227 g) ground sausage

1 large onion, diced

1 poblano chile, stemmed, seeded, and finely chopped

1 (14-ounce / 397-g) can tomato paste

1½ cups grated Cheddar cheese, divided

1 teaspoon seasoned salt

1 teaspoon freshly ground black pepper

1 tablespoon minced garlic

1. Place the peppers in a disposable aluminum pan, wrapping them at the base with aluminum foil rings, if necessary, to keep them stable.

2. Supply your smoker with wood pellets and follow the manufacturer's specific start-up procedure. Preheat, with the lid closed, to 350ºF (177ºC).

3. On your stove top, in a large skillet over medium-high heat, brown the ground beef and ground sausage together for 5 to 7 minutes; drain off the fat and crumble the meat.

4. Stir the onion, poblano chile, tomato paste, 1 cup of Cheddar cheese, salt, pepper, and garlic into the meat, mixing well.

5. Stuff the bell peppers in the aluminum pan with the meat mixture.

6. Place the pan on the grill, close the lid, and smoke for 1 hour.

7. Top the stuffed peppers with the remaining ½ cup of cheese and continue smoking with the lid closed for 15 minutes, then remove from the heat.

8. Serve hot.

Pepper Brisket with Mustard

Prep time: 35 minutes | Cook time: 8 to 10 hours | Serves 8 to 12

1 cup kosher salt

1 cup coarsely ground black pepper

1 (8- to 12-pound / 3.6- to 5.4-kg) brisket, most fat trimmed off

1 cup yellow mustard

1 cup apple cider vinegar

1 cup apple juice

2 tablespoons salt

Pink butcher paper

1. Supply your smoker with wood pellets and follow the manufacturer's specific start-up procedure. Preheat, with the lid closed, to 225ºF (107ºC).

2. In a small bowl, combine the salt and pepper.

3. Slather the trimmed brisket with the mustard, then generously apply the salt and pepper mixture to the meat until it's well coated.

4. Place the meat in the center of the grill, fat-side up. Close the lid and smoke for 4 to 5 hours, or until a meat thermometer inserted in the thickest part of the meat reads 165ºF (74ºC).

5. While the brisket is smoking, make the mop sauce. In a bowl, combine the apple cider vinegar, apple juice, and salt, and pour into a spray bottle.

6. When the brisket has finished the first 4 to 5 hours of cooking, spray it with the mop sauce and wrap tightly with pink butcher paper to seal in the juices. Close the lid and continue smoking for another 4 to 5 hours (or longer as needed), spraying with the mop sauce every hour. You're looking for an internal temperature of 195ºF (91ºC) to 205ºF (96ºC), and the brisket should have a nice dark bark.

7. Remove the meat from the grill, unwrap it, and let rest for up to an hour before slicing.

8. Separate the point side by dividing at the fat line. Shred or reserve for burnt ends.

9. Cut the flat-shaped half of the brisket against the grain into thin slices.

Beef Sausage Meatloaf

Prep time: 30 minutes | Cook time: 2 to 2½ hours | Serves 6 to 8

Meatloaf:

1 pound (454 g) 80% lean ground beef

1 pound (454 g) pork sausage, like Jimmy Dean

2 large eggs

1 cup Italian bread crumbs

½ cup pizza sauce, plus an additional ½ cup, to serve

½ teaspoon garlic salt

½ teaspoon seasoned salt

½ teaspoon ground pepper

½ teaspoon granulated garlic

Pizza Stuffing:

2 tablespoons extra-virgin olive oil

1 cup sliced portobello mushrooms (about 6 small mushrooms)

⅔ cup sliced red onion (1 small onion)

⅔ cup sliced green bell pepper (1 medium green pepper)

½ cup sliced red bell pepper (1 small red pepper)

Pinch of salt and black pepper

2 cups shredded Mozzarella cheese

2 cups shredded Cheddar or Jack cheese

3 ounces (85 g) sliced pepperoni sausage

1. In a large bowl, combine the meatloaf ingredients thoroughly using your hands for best results.

2. In a medium skillet, heat the olive oil over medium-high heat and sauté the mushrooms, red onion, green bell pepper, and red bell pepper for about 2 minutes, until the vegetables are al dente. Season the vegetables with a pinch of salt and black pepper. Set aside.

3. On parchment paper, flatten the meatloaf into a 3/8-inch-thick rectangle. Evenly spread the sautéed vegetables over the meat. Top the vegetables with the Mozzarella, followed by the Cheddar or Jack. Top the cheese with the pepperoni.

4. Use the parchment paper to roll the meatloaf, making sure to seal the ends and all seams.

5. Configure your wood pellet-smoker grill for indirect heat and preheat to 225ºF (107ºC) using oak pellets or a blend.

6. Smoke the stuffed pizza meatloaf for 1 hour.

7. After an hour, increase the pit temperature to 350ºF (177ºC), and cook until the internal temperature of the stuffed pizza meatloaf reaches 170ºF (77ºC).

8. Top the meatloaf with the remaining ½ cup pizza sauce and let rest under a loose foiled tent for 15 minutes before serving.

Beef and Rice Stuffed Peppers

Prep time: 30 minutes | Cook time: 1 hour 30 minutes | Serves 4 to 6

6 to 8 large bell peppers (green, yellow, and red)

1 small red onion

3 celery stalks

2 tablespoons extra-virgin olive oil

1 pound (454 g) 80% lean ground beef

1 (28-ounce / 794-g) can tomato sauce

2 cups cooked white rice

1 teaspoon seasoned salt

½ teaspoon black pepper

2 cloves garlic, minced, or 1 teaspoon crushed garlic

1. Cut off the tops of the bell peppers and save for use in the stuffing. Core and remove the seeds from the peppers.

2. Finely chop the onion, celery, and bell pepper tops.

3. In a 10-inch skillet over medium heat, warm the olive oil and sauté the vegetables for 3 to 4

minutes, until the vegetables are al dente. Remove the vegetables from the pan and set aside.

4. Using same skillet, cook the ground beef over medium heat for 8 to 10 minutes, stirring occasionally, until the beef is brown. Drain the fat.

5. Set aside ½ cup of tomato sauce to top stuffed peppers.

6. Mix the browned ground beef, sautéed vegetables, rice, and remaining tomato sauce in a large bowl. Season with the salt, pepper, and garlic.

7. Loosely stuff the bell peppers with the filling and top them with the remaining tomato sauce.

8. Configure your wood pellet smoker-grill for indirect cooking and preheat to 180ºF (82ºC) using apple or hickory pellets.

9. Smoke the bell peppers for 45 minutes.

10. After 45 minutes, increase the pit temperature to 350ºF (177ºC), and cook for another 45 minutes.

11. Remove the peppers and rest under a foil tent for 10 minutes before serving.

Strip Steaks with Garlic and Oregano

Prep time: 10 minutes | Cook time: 15 minutes | Serves 2

2 USDA Choice or Prime 1¼- to 1½-inch-thick New York strip steaks (about 12 to 14 ounces / 340 to 397 g each)

Extra-virgin olive oil

4 teaspoons Garlic and Oregano Rub or salt and pepper, divided

1. Remove the steaks from the refrigerator and cover loosely with plastic wrap about 45 minutes before cooking to bring them to room temperature.

2. Once the steaks reach room temperature, brush them on both sides with olive oil.

3. Season each side of the steaks with 1 teaspoon of the rub or salt and pepper, and then let stand at room temperature for at least 5 minutes before grilling.

4. Configure your wood pellet smoker-grill for direct cooking by using searing grates, set the temperature to high, and preheat to at least 450ºF (232ºC) using any pellets.

5. Place the steaks on the grill and cook on one side until slightly charred, 2 to 3 minutes.

6. On the same side, rotate the steaks 90 degrees for cross grill marks, and cook for an additional 2 to 3 minutes.

7. Flip the steaks over and grill until they reach desired doneness: 3 to 5 minutes for medium rare (an internal temperature of 135ºF / 57ºC), 6 to 7 minutes for medium (an internal temperature of 140ºF / 60ºC), 8 to 10 minutes for medium-well (an internal temperature of 150ºF / 66ºC).

8. Transfer the steaks to a platter, tent loosely with foil, and let rest 5 minutes before serving.

Tri-Tip Roast

Prep time: 20 minutes | Cook time: 2 hours | Serves 4 to 6

1 (2½- to 3-pound/ 1.1- to 1.4-kg) whole peeled tri-tip roast

3 tablespoons roasted garlic–flavored extra-virgin olive oil

3 tablespoons Garlic and Oregano Rub or your favorite Santa Maria–style rub

1. Rub all sides of the tri-tip with the olive oil and then with the Garlic and Oregano Rub or other rub.

2. Double-wrap the seasoned tri-tip roast with plastic wrap and refrigerate overnight.

3. Configure your wood pellet smoker-grill for indirect heat and preheat to 180ºF (82ºC) using hickory pellets or a blend.

4. If your unit has one, insert your wood pellet smoker-grill meat probe into the thickest part of the tri-tip roast and smoke for 1 hour.

5. After an hour, increase the pit temperature to 325ºF (163ºC). Cook until the internal temperature reaches 140ºF (60ºC) to 145ºF (63ºC).

6. Rest the smoked tri-tip under a loose foil tent for 15 minutes before serving.

Beef Chuck Short Ribs

Prep time: 20 minutes | Cook time: 5 to 6 hours | Serves 2 to 4

English-cut 4-bone slab beef chuck short ribs

3 to 4 tablespoons yellow mustard or extra-virgin olive oil

3 to 5 tablespoons Garlic and Oregano Rub

1. Trim the fat cap from the ribs, leaving a ¼ inch fat, and remove any silver skin.

2. Remove the membrane from the bones to season the meat properly by working a spoon handle under the membrane to get a piece lifted. Use a paper towel to grab the membrane and pull it off the bones.

3. Slather the mustard or olive oil on all sides of the short rib slab. Season liberally on all sides with the rub.

4. Configure your wood pellet smoker-grill for indirect heat and preheat to 225ºF (107ºC) using mesquite or hickory pellets.

5. Insert your wood pellet smoker-grill or a remote meat probe into the thickest part of the slab of ribs. If your grill does not have meat probe capabilities or you don't own a remote meat probe, then use an instant-read digital

thermometer during the cook for internal temperature readings.

6. Place the short ribs bone-side down on the grill and smoke at 225ºF (107ºC) for 5 hours.

7. If after 5 hours the ribs have not reached an internal temperature of at least 195ºF (91ºC), then increase the pit temperature to 250ºF (121ºC) until the internal temperature reaches 195ºF (91ºC) to 205ºF (96ºC).

8. Rest the smoked short ribs under a loose foil tent for 15 minutes before serving.

Tri-Tip Roast

Prep time: 15 minutes | Cook time: 1 hour 15 minutes | Serves 4

1 (2- to 3-pound / 0.9- to 1.4-kg) tri-tip roast

2 tablespoons ancho chile powder

2 tablespoons finely ground coffee beans

5 teaspoons dark brown sugar

1 tablespoon hot smoked Spanish paprika

1½ teaspoons dried oregano

1½ teaspoons freshly ground black pepper

1½ teaspoons ground coriander

1½ teaspoons mustard powder

1 teaspoon chile de árbol powder or ¾ teaspoon finely ground red pepper flakes

1 teaspoon ground ginger

1 tablespoon kosher salt, plus more as needed

1. A tri-tip roast will usually have a fat cap on one side and silver skin on the other. If the butcher has not already trimmed these, remove them with a knife.

2. Mix the ancho chile powder, ground coffee, brown sugar, paprika, oregano, pepper, coriander, mustard powder, chile de árbol powder, ginger and the salt in a small bowl. Season both sides of the roast evenly with the spice rub (save any extra rub for your next cook). Place the roast on a wire

rack set inside a rimmed baking sheet and chill uncovered for 3 to 6 hours.

3. Let the roast sit for 1 hour to come to room temperature, which will help it cook quickly and more evenly.

4. Prepare your Traeger by turning it to the SMOKE setting. Wait about 5 minutes for it to produce smoke, then set the Traeger to run at 275ºF (135ºC).

5. Place the baking sheet with the roast on your Traeger and cook for 1 hour or until the internal temperature reaches 130ºF (54ºC). Remove the roast from the Traeger and turn it up to the highest setting. When your Traeger is up to temperature on its highest setting, remove the roast from the pan and place it directly on the grill for 3 minutes per side to achieve a nice sear. The internal temperature will be approximately 140ºF (60ºC). Let the roast rest for 15 minutes before slicing. You will want to slice the tri-tip across the grain in ¼-inch-thick slices.

Mustard Beef Brisket

Prep time: 5 minutes | Cook time: 11 to 14 hours | Makes 15 to 20 pieces

1 (12- to 15-pound / 5.4- to 6.8-kg) whole packer brisket

1 cup yellow mustard

½ cup kosher salt

½ cup ground black pepper, café grind

1. Trim the fat cap off the top of the brisket and remove all silver skin. We also like to trim the sides of the brisket to square it up so there will be an even cook. Trim the bottom fat cap to about a ¼ inch thickness. This excess fat will provide moisture throughout your cook.

2. Rub the entire brisket with the yellow mustard. The mustard will act as a binder for the salt and pepper rub. It doesn't have to be perfect; the mustard will have no effect on your cook. In a small bowl, combine the salt and pepper and mix well. If you have an empty shaker bottle/dredge you could use that as well. When evenly mixed, apply an even layer of the salt-and-pepper mixture over the brisket. Make sure to turn the brisket over and apply the salt and pepper to the fat cap side as well.

3. Meanwhile, prepare your Traeger by turning it to the SMOKE setting. Wait about 5 minutes for it to produce smoke, then set the Traeger to run at 225ºF (107ºC).

4. Place the brisket directly on the grill grate, fat-side down, and cook for 8 hours. After 8 hours, take a temperature reading of the brisket once in the point area and once in the flat. If the temperature is not at 160ºF (71ºC), close the lid and monitor the temperature every 30 minutes. When the brisket registers to 160ºF (71ºC), double wrap it with foil or butcher paper. Place the wrapped brisket back on the grill grate and continue to cook for another 3 hours.

5. After 3 hours, test for doneness. While most assess doneness by a certain temperature, we like to go by feel. Using a toothpick or the end of your thermometer, you should be able to penetrate the brisket with little resistance. It should feel almost as though you are putting the toothpick or thermometer probe through a warm stick of butter. Ideally the internal temperature you should find for this level of tenderness is 205ºF (96ºC).

6. When done, remove the brisket from the grill; let the foil or butcher paper vent for 3 to 5 minutes to stop the cooking process. Then, close the wrapping and wrap the brisket in a towel and place it in an empty cooler to rest for at least an

hour. When ready to serve, slice the brisket across the grain. Each slice should be roughly a ¼ inch thick. Pitmasters often think of this as being the thickness of a #2 pencil.

Corned Beef Brisket

Prep time: 5 minutes | Cook time: 4½ to 5 hours | Serves 8 to 10

3 to 4 pounds (1.4 to 1.8 kg) corned beef brisket flat

8 ounces (227 g) coarse or whole grain mustard

⅓ cup your favorite BBQ rub

1.   Prepare your Traeger by turning it to the SMOKE setting. Wait about 5 minutes for it to produce smoke, then set the Traeger to run at 225ºF (107ºC).

2.   Discard the seasoning packet that comes with the corned beef brisket. Making sure the fat cap side is down, apply a coat of mustard to the top and sides of the brisket. Next, apply a coat of BBQ rub onto the top and sides of the brisket. Making sure you keep the fat cap–side up, place the brisket into an aluminum pan. Place on the Traeger.

3.   Allow the meat to cook for 2½ hours or until it reaches 140ºF (60ºC) in the thickest part. Then cover the aluminum pan with foil to allow the meat to braise for the remainder of the cook.

4.   Allow the brisket to cook for an additional 2 to 2½ hours, until it has an internal temperature of 185ºF (85ºC). Remove the roast and let it rest for 30 minutes before carving. Make sure you remember to slice across the grain.

Skirt Steak with Mango

Prep time: 15 minutes | Cook time: 10 minutes | Serves 6 to 8
Marinade:

½ cup olive oil

2 tablespoons Worcestershire sauce

2 tablespoons lime juice

2 tablespoons lemon juice

6 cloves garlic, minced

1 tablespoon chili powder

1 tablespoon dried cumin

1 (1- to 2-pound / 454- to 907-g) skirt steak, trimmed

Mango Chimichurri:

¼ cup packed flat-leaf parsley

½ cup packed cilantro

1 shallot, peeled

2 cloves garlic, peeled

2 mangoes, peeled, pitted and finely chopped

½ cup olive oil

2 tablespoons white vinegar

Salt and pepper, to taste

1.   To make the marinade, in a medium bowl, whisk together the olive oil, Worcestershire sauce, lime juice, lemon juice, garlic, chili powder and cumin and pour into a plastic freezer bag or shallow container. Add the skirt steak and marinate for at least 6 hours or preferably overnight in the refrigerator.

2.   To make the chimichurri, finely chop the parsley, cilantro, shallot and garlic in a food processor. Scrape into a bowl and stir in the mangos, olive oil, vinegar, salt and pepper. Allow the mixture to sit, covered, for 2 to 4 hours before serving to allow flavors to meld. You can also make the chimichurri the day before; after marinating, chill in the refrigerator, then allow to return to room temperature before serving.

3.   Set your Traeger to run at the highest setting. Let it run for 15 minutes to preheat properly. Remove the steak from the marinade and dry with a paper towel. Grill for 5 minutes per side

or until an internal temperature of 140ºF (60ºC) is achieved.

4. Transfer the steak to a cutting board and loosely tent it with foil and let it rest for 5 to 10 minutes. Slice across the grain and top with the mango chimichurri.

Beef Roast with Allspice

Prep time: 5 minutes | Cook time: 4 to 6 hours | Serves 6

4 pounds (1.8 kg) beef roast boneless

1 (11-ounce / 312-g) can beef stock

½ ounce (14 g) allspice

1. Combine the beef stock and dry salad dressing mix in a bowl.

2. Pour this mixture evenly over beef.

3. Load the wood tray with one small handful of hickory pellets and preheat the smoker to 250ºF (121ºC). Add the tray to the smoker.

4. Smoke beef for approximately 4 to 6 hours.

5. Your beef is ready when internal temperature reaches 150ºF (66ºC) to 160ºF (71ºC).

6. Remove from smoker and let rest for 15 minutes.

7. Slice and serve warm.

Beef Brisket with Sauce

Prep time: 10 minutes | Cook time: 5 hours | Serves 8

4 pounds (1.8 kg) beef brisket

⅔ cup soy sauce or tamari sauce

⅔ cup water

¼ cup dry white wine

2 teaspoons fresh lemon juice

¼ cup brown sugar

½ teaspoon garlic powder

½ teaspoon ground ginger

1. In a container, combine all ingredients for the marinade. Place in the beef and marinate overnight.

2. Remove the beef from marinade and pat dry on a kitchen towel.

3. Start the pellet grill on SMOKE with the lid open until the fire is established. Set the temperature to 250ºF (121ºC) and preheat, lid closed, for 10 to 15 minutes.

4. Smoke from 4 to 5 hours. After the roast has been in the smoker for around 3 hours check the internal temperature. You are looking for a temperature of 150ºF (66ºC) to 160ºF (71ºC).

5. Remove from Smoker and let cool for 10 to 15 minutes.

Beef Roast Barbacoa

Prep time: 15 minutes | Cook time: 3 hours | Serves 12

1½ teaspoons pepper

1 tablespoon dried oregano

1½ teaspoons cayenne pepper

1½ teaspoons chili powder

1½ teaspoons garlic powder

1 teaspoon ground cumin

1 teaspoon salt

3 pounds (1.4 kg) boneless beef chuck roast

1. Add dampened hickory wood to your smoker and preheat to 200ºF (93ºC).

2. Take a small bowl and add oregano, cayenne pepper, black pepper, garlic powder, chili powder, cumin, salt, and seasoned salt.

3. Mix well.

4. Dip the chuck roast into your mixing bowl and rub the spice mix all over.

5. Transfer the meat to your smoker and smoker for 1½ hours.

6.   Make sure to turn the meat after every 30 minutes, if you see less smoke formation, add more pellets after every 30 minutes as well.

7.   Once the meat shows a dark red color with darkened edges, transfer the meat to a roasting pan and seal it tightly with an aluminum foil.

8.   Preheat your oven to 325ºF (163ºC).

9.   Transfer the meat to your oven and bake for 1½ hours more.

10.   Shred the meat using two forks and serve.

Beef Ribs with Mustard

Prep time: 20 minutes | Cook time: 1 hour 20 minutes | Serves 4

½ cup Dijon mustard

2 tablespoons cider vinegar

3 pounds (1.4 kg) spareribs

4 tablespoons paprika powder

½ tablespoon chili powder

1½ tablespoons garlic powder

2 teaspoons ground cumin

2 teaspoons onion powder

1½ tablespoons ground black pepper

2 tablespoons salt

2 tablespoons butter, optional

1.   Preheat a Wood Pellet Smoker and Grill to 350ºF (177ºC), using a small mixing bowl, add in the mustard and the vinegar then mix properly to combine. Rub the mixture on the spareribs, coating all sides. Using another mixing bowl, add in the paprika powder, chili powder, garlic powder, cumin, onion powder, salt, and pepper to taste then mix properly to combine.

2.   Reserve a small quantity of the mixture, seasoned the spareribs with the rest of the spice mixture, coating all sides. Wrap the seasoned ribs in aluminum foil, top with the butter if desired then place the ribs on the preheated grill.

3.   Grill the ribs for about one hour until it is cooked through. Make sure you flip after every twenty minutes. Once the ribs are cooked through, remove from the grill, unwrap the aluminum foil then grill the ribs for another two to five minutes until crispy.

4.   Let the ribs cool for a few minutes, slice, and serve.

Aromatic Back Ribs

Prep time: 15 minutes | Cook time: 1 hour 30 minutes | Serves 6

2 racks baby back ribs

¾ cup chicken broth

¾ cup soy sauce

1 cup sugar

6 tablespoons cider vinegar

6 tablespoons olive oil

3 minced garlic cloves

2 teaspoons salt

1 tablespoon paprika

½ teaspoon chili powder

½ teaspoon pepper to taste

¼ teaspoon garlic powder

Dash of cayenne pepper

Barbecue sauce

1.   Using a large mixing bowl, add in half of the sugar, soy sauce, vinegar, oil, and garlic then mix properly to combine. This makes the marinade. Place the pork ribs in a Ziploc bag, pour in about ⅔ of the prepared marinade then sake properly to coat. Let the ribs marinate in the refrigerator overnight.

2.   Using another mixing bowl, add in the rest of the sugar, salt, and seasonings on the list then mix properly to combine. Rub the ribs with the mixture, coating all sides then set aside. Preheat a Wood Pellet Smoker Grill to 250ºF (121ºC),

place the ribs on the preheated grill and grill for about two hours.

3.   Blast the ribs with the reserved marinade and cook for an additional one hour. Once cooked, let rest for about five to ten minutes, slice, and serve.

Beef Brisket with BBQ Sauce

Prep time: 30 minutes | Cook time: 6 hours | Serves 8 to 10

1 (6-pound / 2.7-kg) brisket point
2 tablespoons yellow mustard
1 batch Brown Sugar Rub
2 tablespoons honey
1 cup barbecue sauce
2 tablespoons light brown sugar

1.   Supply your smoker with wood pellets and follow the manufacturer's specific start-up procedure. Preheat the grill, with the lid closed, to 225ºF (107ºC).

2.   Using a boning knife, carefully remove all but about ½ inch of the large layer of fat covering one side of your brisket point.

3.   Coat the point all over with mustard and season it with the rub. Using your hands, work the rub into the meat.

4.   Place the point directly on the grill grate and smoke until its internal temperature reaches 165ºF (74ºC).

5.   Pull the brisket from the grill and wrap it completely in aluminum foil or butcher paper.

6.   Increase the grill's temperature to 350ºF (177ºC) and return the wrapped brisket to it. Continue to cook until its internal temperature reaches 185ºF (85ºC).

7.   Remove the point from the grill, unwrap it, and cut the meat into 1-inch cubes. Place the cubes in an aluminum pan and stir in the honey, barbecue sauce, and brown sugar.

8.   Place the pan in the grill and smoke the beef cubes for 1 hour more, uncovered. Remove the burnt ends from the grill and serve immediately.

Tri-Tip Roast

Prep time: 10 minutes | Cook time: 2 or 3 hours | Serves 4

1½ pounds (680 g) tri-tip roast
1 batch Espresso Brisket Rub

1.   Supply your smoker with wood pellets and follow the manufacturer's specific start-up procedure. Preheat the grill, with the lid closed, to 180ºF (82ºC).

2.   Season the tri-tip roast with the rub. Using your hands, work the rub into the meat.

3.   Place the roast directly on the grill grate and smoke until its internal temperature reaches 140ºF (60ºC).

4.   Increase the grill's temperature to 450ºF (232ºC) and continue to cook until the roast's internal temperature reaches 145ºF (63ºC). This same technique can be done over an open flame or in a cast-iron skillet with some butter.

5.   Remove the tri-tip roast from the grill and let it rest 10 to 15 minutes, before slicing and serving.

Tri-Tip Roast with Garlic

Prep time: 25 minutes | Cook time: 5 hours | Serves 4

1½ pounds (680 g) tri-tip roast
Salt and freshly ground black pepper, to taste
2 teaspoons garlic powder
2 teaspoons lemon pepper
½ cup apple juice

1.   Supply your smoker with wood pellets and follow the manufacturer's specific start-up procedure. Preheat the grill, with the lid closed, to 180ºF (82ºC).

2.   Season the tri-tip roast with salt, pepper, garlic powder, and lemon pepper. Using your hands, work the seasoning into the meat.

3.   Place the roast directly on the grill grate and smoke for 4 hours.

4.   Pull the tri-tip from the grill and place it on enough aluminum foil to wrap it completely.

5.   Increase the grill's temperature to 375ºF (191ºC).

6.   Fold in three sides of the foil around the roast and add the apple juice. Fold in the last side, completely enclosing the tri-tip and liquid. Return the wrapped tri-tip to the grill and cook for 45 minutes more.

7.   Remove the tri-tip roast from the grill and let it rest for 10 to 15 minutes, before unwrapping, slicing, and serving.

Beef with Mustard

Prep time: 25 minutes | Cook time: 12 to 14 hours | Serves 5 to 8

1 (4-pound / 1.8-kg) top round roast

2 tablespoons yellow mustard

1 batch Espresso Brisket Rub

½ cup beef broth

1.   Supply your smoker with wood pellets and follow the manufacturer's specific start-up procedure. Preheat the grill, with the lid closed, to 225ºF (107ºC).

2.   Coat the top round roast all over with mustard and season it with the rub. Using your hands, work the rub into the meat.

3.   Place the roast directly on the grill grate and smoke until its internal temperature reaches 160ºF (71ºC) and a dark bark has formed.

4.   Pull the roast from the grill and place it on enough aluminum foil to wrap it completely.

5.   Increase the grill's temperature to 350ºF (177ºC).

6.   Fold in three sides of the foil around the roast and add the beef broth. Fold in the last side, completely enclosing the roast and liquid. Return the wrapped roast to the grill and cook until its internal temperature reaches 195ºF (91ºC).

7.   Pull the roast from the grill and place it in a cooler. Cover the cooler and let the roast rest for 1 or 2 hours.

8.   Remove the roast from the cooler and unwrap it. Pull apart the beef using just your fingers. Serve immediately.

Beef Roast with Butter

Prep time: 10 minutes | Cook time: 12 to 14 hours | Serves 5 to 8

1 (4-pound / 1.8-kg) top round roast

1 batch Espresso Brisket Rub

1 tablespoon butter

1.   Supply your smoker with wood pellets and follow the manufacturer's specific start-up procedure. Preheat the grill, with the lid closed, to 180ºF (82ºC).

2.   Season the top round roast with the rub. Using your hands, work the rub into the meat.

3.   Place the roast directly on the grill grate and smoke until its internal temperature reaches 140ºF (60ºC). Remove the roast from the grill.

4.   Place a cast-iron skillet on the grill grate and increase the grill's temperature to 450ºF (232ºC). Place the roast in the skillet, add the butter, and cook until its internal temperature reaches 145ºF

(63ºC), flipping once after about 3 minutes. (I recommend reverse-searing the meat over an open flame rather than in the cast-iron skillet, if your grill has that option.)

5.   Remove the roast from the grill and let it rest for 10 to 15 minutes, before slicing and serving.

Rib Roast

Prep time: 15 minutes | Cook time: 4 or 5 hours | Serves 4 to 6

1 (3-bone) rib roast
Salt and freshly ground black pepper, to taste
1 garlic clove, minced

1.   Supply your smoker with wood pellets and follow the manufacturer's specific start-up procedure. Preheat the grill, with the lid closed, to 360ºF (182ºC).

2.   Season the roast all over with salt and pepper and, using your hands, rub it all over with the minced garlic.

3.   Place the roast directly on the grill grate and smoke for 4 or 5 hours, until its internal temperature reaches 145ºF (63ºC) for medium-rare.

4.   Remove the roast from the grill and let it rest for 15 minutes, before slicing and serving.

CHAPTER 5: LAMB

Lamb Chops with Pepper Jelly

Prep time: 15 minutes | Cook time: 10 to 20 minutes | Serves 4 to 6

½ cup rice wine vinegar

1 teaspoon liquid smoke

2 tablespoons extra-virgin olive oil

2 tablespoons dried minced onion

1 tablespoon chopped fresh mint

8 (4-ounce / 113-g) lamb chops

½ cup hot pepper jelly

1 tablespoon Sriracha

1 teaspoon salt

1 teaspoon freshly ground black pepper

1. In a small bowl, whisk together the rice wine vinegar, liquid smoke, olive oil, minced onion, and mint. Place the lamb chops in an aluminum roasting pan. Pour the marinade over the meat, turning to coat thoroughly. Cover with plastic wrap and marinate in the refrigerator for 2 hours.

2. Supply your smoker with wood pellets and follow the manufacturer's specific start-up procedure. Preheat, with the lid closed, to 165ºF (74ºC), or the "Smoke" setting.

3. On the stove top, in a small saucepan over low heat, combine the hot pepper jelly and Sriracha and keep warm.

4. When ready to cook the chops, remove them from the marinade and pat dry. Discard the marinade.

5. Season the chops with the salt and pepper, then place them directly on the grill grate, close the lid, and smoke for 5 minutes to "breathe" some smoke into them.

6. Remove the chops from the grill. Increase the pellet cooker temperature to 450ºF (232ºC), or the "High" setting. Once the grill is up to temperature, place the chops on the grill and sear, cooking for 2 minutes per side to achieve medium-rare chops. A meat thermometer inserted in the thickest part of the meat should read 145ºF (63ºC). Continue grilling, if necessary, to your desired doneness.

7. Serve the chops with the warm Sriracha pepper jelly on the side.

Garlicky Lamb with Basil

Prep time: 30 minutes | Cook time: 1 to 2 hours | Serves 4

2 racks of lamb, trimmed, frenched, and tied into a crown

1¼ cups extra-virgin olive oil, divided

2 tablespoons chopped fresh basil

2 tablespoons chopped fresh rosemary

2 tablespoons ground sage

2 tablespoons ground thyme

8 garlic cloves, minced

2 teaspoons salt

2 teaspoons freshly ground black pepper

1. Set the lamb out on the counter to take the chill off, about an hour.

2. In a small bowl, combine 1 cup of olive oil, the basil, rosemary, sage, thyme, garlic, salt, and pepper.

3. Baste the entire crown with the herbed olive oil and wrap the exposed frenched bones in aluminum foil.

4. Supply your smoker with wood pellets and follow the manufacturer's specific start-up procedure. Preheat, with the lid closed, to 275ºF (135ºC).

5. Put the lamb directly on the grill, close the lid, and smoke for 1 hour 30 minutes to 2 hours, or until a meat thermometer inserted in the thickest part reads 140ºF (60ºC).

6. Remove the lamb from the heat, tent with foil, and let rest for about 15 minutes before serving. The temperature will rise about 5ºF during the rest period, for a finished temperature of 145ºF (63ºC).

Lamb Gyro with Tomato

Prep time: 20 minutes | Cook time: 40 minutes | Serves 4

1 pound (454 g) ground lamb

2 teaspoons salt

1 teaspoon freshly ground black pepper

2 tablespoons chopped fresh oregano

1 tablespoon minced garlic

1 tablespoon onion powder

4 to 6 pocketless pitas

Tzatziki sauce, for serving

1 tomato, chopped, for serving

1 small onion, thinly sliced, for serving

1. In a medium bowl, combine the lamb, salt, pepper, oregano, garlic, and onion powder; mix well. Cover with plastic wrap and refrigerate overnight.

2. Supply your smoker with wood pellets and follow the manufacturer's specific start-up procedure. Preheat, with the lid closed, to 300ºF (149ºC).

3. Remove the meat mixture from the refrigerator and, on a Frogmat or a piece of heavy-duty aluminum foil, roll and shape it into a rectangular loaf about 8 inches long by 5 inches wide.

4. Place the loaf directly on the grill, close the lid, and smoke for 35 minutes, or until a meat

thermometer inserted in the center reads 155ºF (68ºC).

5. Remove the loaf from the heat and increase the temperature to 450ºF (232ºC).

6. Cut the loaf into ⅛-inch slices and place on a Frogmat or a piece of heavy-duty foil.

7. Return the meat (still on the Frogmat or foil) to the smoker, close the lid, and continue cooking for 2 to 4 minutes, or until the edges are crispy.

8. Warm the pitas in the smoker for a few minutes and serve with the lamb, tzatziki sauce, chopped tomato, and sliced onion.

Vinegary Lamb Leg

Prep time: 15 minutes | Cook time: 20 to 25 minutes | Serves 12 to 16

2 tablespoons finely chopped fresh rosemary

1 tablespoon ground thyme

5 garlic cloves, minced

2 tablespoons sea salt

1 tablespoon freshly ground black pepper

Butcher's string

1 (6- to 8-pound / 2.7- to 3.6-kg) whole boneless leg of lamb

¼ cup extra-virgin olive oil

1 cup red wine vinegar

½ cup canola oil

1. In a small bowl, combine the rosemary, thyme, garlic, salt, and pepper; set aside.

2. Using butcher's string, tie the leg of lamb into the shape of a roast. Your butcher should also be happy to truss the leg for you.

3. Rub the lamb generously with the olive oil and season with the spice mixture. Transfer to a plate, cover with plastic wrap, and refrigerate for 4 hours.

4. Remove the lamb from the refrigerator but do not rinse.

5. Supply your smoker with wood pellets and follow the manufacturer's specific start-up procedure. Preheat, with the lid closed, to 325ºF (163ºC).

6. In a small bowl, combine the red wine vinegar and canola oil for basting.

7. Place the lamb directly on the grill, close the lid, and smoke for 20 to 25 minutes per pound (depending on desired doneness), basting with the oil and vinegar mixture every 30 minutes. Lamb is generally served medium-rare to medium, so it will be done when a meat thermometer inserted in the thickest part reads 140ºF (60ºC) to 145ºF (63ºC).

8. Let the lamb rest for about 15 minutes before slicing to serve.

Rosemary Lamb Chops

Prep time: 15 minutes | Cook time: 2 hours 5 minutes | Serves 4

4½ pounds (2.0 kg) bone-in lamb chops
2 tablespoons olive oil
Salt and freshly ground black pepper , to taste
1 bunch fresh rosemary

1. Supply your smoker with wood pellets and follow the manufacturer's specific start-up procedure. Preheat the grill, with the lid closed, to 180ºF (82ºC).

2. Rub the lamb chops all over with olive oil and season on both sides with salt and pepper.

3. Spread the rosemary directly on the grill grate, creating a surface area large enough for all the chops to rest on. Place the chops on the rosemary and smoke until they reach an internal temperature of 135ºF (57ºC).

4. Increase the grill's temperature to 450ºF (232ºC), remove the rosemary, and continue to cook the chops until their internal temperature reaches 145ºF (63ºC).

5. Remove the chops from the grill and let them rest for 5 minutes before serving.

Rosemary Rack of Lamb

Prep time: 25 minutes | Cook time: 4 to 6 hours | Serves 6

1 (2-pound / 907-g) rack of lamb
1 batch Rosemary Lamb Seasoning

1. Supply your smoker with wood pellets and follow the manufacturer's specific start-up procedure. Preheat the grill, with the lid closed, to 225ºF (107ºC).

2. Using a boning knife, score the bottom fat portion of the rib meat.

3. Using your hands, rub the rack of lamb all over with the seasoning, making sure it penetrates into the scored fat.

4. Place the rack directly on the grill grate, fat-side up, and smoke until its internal temperature reaches 145ºF (63ºC).

5. Remove the rack from the grill and let it rest for 20 to 30 minutes, before slicing it into individual ribs to serve.

Rack of Lamb with Walnut

Prep time: 25 minutes | Cook time: 1 hour 30 minutes | Serves 4

3 tablespoons Dijon mustard
2 garlic cloves, minced, or 2 teaspoons crushed garlic
½ teaspoon garlic powder
½ teaspoon kosher salt
½ teaspoon black pepper
½ teaspoon rosemary
1 (1½ to 2-pound / 680- to 907-g) rack of lamb, Frenched

1 cup crushed walnuts

1. Combine the mustard, garlic, garlic powder, salt, pepper, and rosemary in a small bowl.

2. Spread the seasoning mix evenly on all sides of the lamb and sprinkle with the crushed walnuts. Press the walnuts lightly with your hand to adhere the nuts to the meat.

3. Wrap the walnut-crusted rack of lamb loosely with plastic wrap and refrigerate overnight to allow the seasonings to penetrate the meat.

4. Remove the walnut crusted rack of lamb from the refrigerator and rest for 30 minutes to allow it to come to room temperature.

5. Configure your wood pellet smoker-grill for indirect cooking and preheat to 225°F (107°C) using apple pellets.

6. Place the rack of lamb bone-side down directly on the grill.

7. Smoke at 225°F (107°C) until the thickest part of the rack of lamb reaches the desired internal temperature, measured with a digital instant-read thermometer, as you near the times listed in the chart.

8. Rest the lamb under a loose foil tent for 5 minutes before serving.

Lamb Leg with Parsley

Prep time: 20 minutes | Cook time: 1½ to 2 hours | Serves 8

1 (4-pound / 1.8-kg) boneless leg of lamb

½ cup roasted garlic–flavored extra-virgin olive oil

¼ cup dried parsley

3 garlic cloves, minced

2 tablespoons fresh-squeezed lemon juice or 1 tablespoon lemon zest (from 1 medium lemon)

2 tablespoons dried oregano

1 tablespoon dried rosemary

½ teaspoon black pepper

1. Remove any netting from the leg of lamb. Trim any large pieces of gristle, silver skin, and fat.

2. In a small bowl, combine the olive oil, parsley, garlic, lemon juice or zest, oregano, rosemary, and pepper.

3. Apply the spice rub on the inner and outer surfaces of the boneless leg of lamb.

4. Use silicone food-grade cooking bands or butcher's twine to secure the boneless leg of lamb. Use bands or twine to form and maintain the lamb's basic shape.

5. Wrap the lamb loosely with plastic wrap and refrigerate overnight to allow the seasonings to penetrate the meat.

6. Remove the lamb from the refrigerator and let it stand at room temperature for an hour.

7. Configure your wood pellet smoker-grill for indirect cooking and preheat to 400°F (204°C) using your pellets of choice.

8. Remove the plastic wrap from the lamb.

9. Insert your wood pellet smoker-grill meat probe or a remote meat probe into the thickest part of the lamb. If your grill does not have meat probe capabilities or you don't own a remote meat probe then use an instant-read digital thermometer during the cook for internal temperature readings. Roast the lamb at 400°F (204°C) until the internal temperature at the thickest part reaches desired doneness.

10. Rest the lamb under a loose foil tent for 10 minutes before carving against the grain and serving.

Rosemary Lamb with Garlic

Prep time: 5 minutes | Cook time: 5 minutes | Serves 2

3 cloves garlic

2 sprigs rosemary

2 tablespoons chopped fresh parsley

1 tablespoon chopped fresh oregano

1 tablespoon chopped fresh thyme

¼ cup olive oil

1 rack of lamb

Salt and pepper, to taste

1.   In a food processor or blender, combine the garlic, rosemary, parsley, oregano, thyme and olive oil until a smooth paste forms.

2.   Slice the lamb into individual chops. Some people like to trim away all the fat from the long part of the bone, but I find that to be quite tasty so I leave it on. Sprinkle both sides of the lamb with salt and pepper. Rub the herb mixture onto the lamb chops and set aside to marinate for 1 hour.

3.   Prepare your Traeger to run on HIGH.

4.   Grill the chops on the Traeger with the lid open for 2 minutes, then flip and cook the chops another 3 minutes on the other side. Chops will be 145ºF (63ºC) for medium rare, or 160ºF (71ºC) for medium. Allow the chops to rest 5 minutes before serving.

Lemony Lamb with Bay Leaves

Prep time: 15 minutes | Cook time: 3 hours | Serves 6

3 pounds (1.4 kg) lamb chops

½ cup olive oil

1 tablespoon salt or to taste

1 cup water

6 bay leaves crushed

2 cloves crushed garlic

1 lemon juice (freshly squeezed)

1.   Combine all ingredients and rub well lamb chops.

2.   Place lamb chops into a container and refrigerate overnight.

3.   Start the pellet grill on SMOKE (recommended apple, oak pellet) with the lid open until the fire is established. Set the temperature to 250ºF (121ºC) and preheat, lid closed, for 10 to 15 minutes.

4.   Smoke lamb chops for 3 hours.

5.   Remove from smoker and let rest for 15 minutes.

6.   Serve.

Lamb Chops with Basil

Prep time: 15 minutes | Cook time: 3 hours 15 minutes | Serves 8

12 lamb chops

Salt and ground black pepper, to taste

4 cloves garlic, finely chopped

3 tablespoons fresh basil, finely chopped

3 teaspoons fresh marjoram leaves, finely chopped

3 teaspoons fresh thyme leaves, finely chopped

1.   Sprinkle lamb chops lightly with the salt and pepper.

2.   In a bowl, combine fresh herbs and garlic; generously rub into chops.

3.   Wrap well, and chill at least 2 hours.

4.   Start the pellet grill on SMOKE with the lid open until the fire is established. Set the temperature to 250ºF (121ºC) and preheat, lid closed, for 10 to 15 minutes.

5.   Place chops on grill racks and smoke for 3 hours.

6.   Allow resting for 10 to 15 minutes before serving.

Lamb Skewers with Lemon

Prep time: 15 minutes | Cook time: 1 hour 15 minutes | Serves 6

2 pounds (907 g) lamb meat without bones, cut into chunks

Marinade:

⅓ cup garlic-infused olive oil

Juice of 1 lime or lemon

1 onion finely chopped

1 teaspoon fresh thyme, chopped

½ teaspoon cumin

1 teaspoon fresh rosemary finely chopped

Salt and freshly ground pepper, to taste

1.   Place lamb chunks in the refrigerator for one hour.

2.   Combine all ingredients for the marinade in a large dish or container.

3.   Add the lamb chunks and toss to coat.

4.   Cover with the plastic membrane and refrigerate overnight.

5.   Pat dry the lamb on a kitchen paper.

6.   Start the pellet grill on SMOKE with the lid open until the fire is established. Set the temperature to 225ºF (107ºC) and preheat, lid closed, for 10 to 15 minutes.

7.   Thread the lamb meat on a wooden (wooden skewers have been soaked) or metal skewers.

8.   Place skewers on a grill rack and smoke for 1¼ hours.

9.   Serve hot.

Pepper Lamb Chops

Prep time: 15 minutes | Cook time: 10 to 20 minutes | Serves 4

Marinade:

½ cup rice wine vinegar

1 teaspoon liquid smoke

2 tablespoons extra virgin olive oil

2 tablespoons dried onion, minced

1 tablespoon fresh mint, chopped

Lamb Chops:

8 (4-ounce / 113-g) lamb chops

½ cup hot pepper jelly

1 tablespoon Sriracha

1 teaspoon salt

1 teaspoon freshly ground black pepper

1.   Take a small bowl and whisk in rice wine vinegar, liquid smoke, olive oil, minced onion, and mint.

2.   Add lamb chops in an aluminum roasting pan, pour marinade over meat and turn well to coat.

3.   Cover with plastic wrap and marinate for 2 hours.

4.   Preheat your smoker to 165ºF (74ºC).

5.   Take a small saucepan and place it over low heat, add hot pepper jelly and sriracha, keep it warm.

6.   Once ready to cook chops, remove them from marinade and pat dry.

7.   Discard marinade.

8.   Season chops with salt, pepper, and transfer to the grill grate.

9.   Close and smoke for 5 minutes.

10. Remove chops from grill and increase the temperature to 450ºF (232ºC).

11. Transfer chops to grill and sear for 2 minutes per side until the internal temperature reaches 145ºF (63ºC).

12. Serve chops and enjoy!

Lamb with Mint Sauce

Prep time: 20 minutes | Cook time: 1 hour 15 minutes | Serves 4

Paste:

½ cup olive oil

½ cup dry mustard

¼ cup hot chili powder

2 tablespoons freshly squeezed lemon juice

2 tablespoons onion, minced

1 tablespoon paprika

1 tablespoon dried thyme

1 tablespoon salt

1 American rack of lamb

Mint Sauce:

¼ cup fresh mint leaves, chopped

¼ cup hot water

2 tablespoons apple cider vinegar

2 tablespoons brown sugar

½ teaspoon salt

½ teaspoon fresh ground pepper

1. Take a small bowl and mix in olive oil, mustard, chili powder, lemon juice, onion, paprika, thyme, Worcestershire sauce, salt.

2. Preheat your smoker to 200ºF (93ºC).

3. Rub the paste all over the lamb and transfer to the smoker, smoke for 75 minutes until internal temperature reaches 145ºF (63ºC).

4. Remove lamb from heat and let it rest for a few minutes, serve with mint sauce.

Lamb Ribs with Herb

Prep time: 30 minutes | Cook time: 2 to 3 hours | Serves 4

4 racks Denver-cut lamb ribs (about 1½ pounds / 680 g each)

2 cups tightly packed chopped mixed fresh herbs, including parsley, sage, rosemary, and/or thyme

5 cloves garlic, roughly chopped

1 tablespoon coarse salt

1 tablespoon sweet paprika

2 teaspoons freshly ground black pepper

2 teaspoons sugar

1 teaspoon hot red pepper flakes, or to taste

½ teaspoon ground mace

⅓ to ½ cup vegetable oil, plus extra as needed

1. Prepare the ribs: Place a rack of ribs meat side down on a rimmed baking sheet. Remove the thin, papery membrane from the back of the rack. Turn the ribs over and, using a knife, score a crosshatch pattern on the meat. Make cuts about ½ inch apart and ¼ inch deep. Repeat with the remaining racks. Arrange the racks in a single layer in a baking dish.

2. Place the herbs, garlic, salt, paprika, pepper, sugar, hot red pepper flakes, and mace in a food processor and finely chop. Work in enough oil to obtain a thick paste.

3. Spread the wet rub over the lamb on both sides using a rubber spatula. Smoke the ribs now, or to get more flavor, let them marinate in the refrigerator for 3 hours or overnight.

4. Set up your smoker following the manufacturer's instructions and preheat to 225ºF (107ºC) to 250ºF (121ºC). Add wood as specified by the manufacturer.

5. Place the ribs directly on the rack in the smoker and smoke until tender and the meat shrinks back from the ends of the bones about ½ inch, 2 to 3 hours.

6. Transfer to a cutting board and cut into individual ribs and serve.

CHAPTER 6: CHICKEN

Chili Chicken

Prep time: 10 minutes | Cook time: 3 hours | Serves 4

1 small whole chicken, cut into 8 pieces (2 legs, 2 thighs, 2 wings, 2 breasts)

1 recipe Chili Chicken Rub

1.   Heat a smoker to 250ºF (121ºC).

2.   Wash the chicken pieces thoroughly and pat them dry with paper towels. Apply the chicken rub all over the exposed areas of the chicken pieces. Place the seasoned chicken pieces in a deep aluminum baking pan, and place the pan in the smoker. Cook for 1½ hours.

3.   Remove the wings, wrap them in aluminum foil, and keep them warm in an oven on the lowest setting. Return the rest of the chicken to the smoker and cook for an additional 1½ hours, or until the internal temperature of the white meat reaches 165ºF (74ºC) and the dark meat reaches 180ºF (82ºC).

4.   Remove the pan from the smoker. Allow the chicken to rest, uncovered, for 15 minutes. Then serve immediately.

Bacon Wrapped Chicken Breasts

Prep time: 15 minutes | Cook time: 1 hour | Serves 2 to 4

4 small boneless, skinless chicken breasts (preferably from small chickens, about 1 pound / 454 g total)

1 (12-ounce / 340-g) can Coca-Cola

1 medium white onion, diced

2 cloves garlic, crushed

2 cups Jack's Old South Huney Muney Cluck Rub, or 1 recipe Chili Chicken Rub

8 thin slices smoked bacon

1.   Place the chicken breasts in a shallow dish, and add the Coca-Cola, onion, and garlic. Cover, and refrigerate overnight.

2.   When you are ready to cook the chicken, preheat a smoker to 325ºF (163ºC).

3.   Remove the chicken from the marinade and apply the rub liberally. Wrap each breast in 2 slices of the bacon, securing the slices with toothpicks. Place the breasts in an aluminum baking pan. Place the pan in the smoker and cook the breasts for 1 hour, or until their internal temperature reaches 165ºF (74ºC).

4.   Remove the pan from the smoker and let the breasts rest, uncovered, in the pan for 15 minutes. Then slice the breasts and garnish them with any bacon that fell aside. My motto with this dish: Have a Coke and a breast, then smile.

Smoked Chicken

Prep time: 10 minutes | Cook time: 3 hours | Serves 4

1 small chicken (about 3 pounds / 1.4 kg), giblets removed

4 cups chicken broth

1 (2-ounce / 57-g) packet dry onion soup mix

2 cups Jack's Old South Huney Muney Cluck Rub, or 1 recipe Chili Chicken Rub

2 cups apple juice

1.   Rinse the chicken inside and out, and pat it dry thoroughly. Place the chicken in a deep pan, add the broth and soup mix, and marinate, covered, in the refrigerator overnight.

2.   When you are ready to cook the chicken, preheat a smoker to 250ºF (121ºC).

3. Remove the pan from the refrigerator and discard the marinade. Apply the rub liberally to the chicken. Place the chicken, breast side up, on a meat rack with the handles down so the bird will be raised above the surface of the pans. Set the rack inside a deep aluminum pan. Pour the apple juice into the pan underneath the meat rack. Place the pan in the smoker and cook for 3 hours or until the breast meat reaches 165ºF (74ºC). Remove the chicken from the smoker and allow it to rest on the rack in its pan for 15 minutes. To serve, carve the chicken into individual pieces.

Apple and Bacon Stuffed Chicken

Prep time: 10 minutes | Cook time: 1 hour | Serves 4

1 yellow apple, such as Golden Delicious, peeled, cored, and chopped
6 slices bacon, fried and crumbled
4 large boneless, skinless chicken breasts (at least 12 ounces / 340 g each)
2 cups Jack's Old South Huney Muney Cluck Rub, or 1 recipe Chili Chicken Rub
1 cup apple juice
1. Heat a smoker to 300ºF (149ºC).
2. In a small bowl, combine the chopped apple and bacon.
3. Using a sharp paring knife, cut a pocket about 3 inches deep in the thickest side of each chicken breast. Spoon the apple mixture into the pockets and secure the openings with toothpicks.
4. Apply the rub to the outside of the chicken breasts. Put the breasts in a large aluminum baking pan, and place the pan in the smoker. Cook, spritzing the chicken with apple juice every 15 minutes, for 1 hour or until the internal temperature of each breast reaches 165ºF (74ºC).

5. Remove the pan from the smoker and allow the chicken to rest, loosely covered, for 10 minutes. Serve.

Buttermilk Chicken

Prep time: 20 minutes | Cook time: 20 minutes | Serves 4

2 cups all-purpose flour
1 tablespoon salt
2 tablespoons finely ground black pepper
1 teaspoon garlic powder
1 teaspoon onion powder
1 teaspoon chili powder
1 teaspoon sugar
1 teaspoon smoked sweet paprika
2 eggs
4 cups buttermilk
1 small chicken (about 3 pounds / 1.4 kg), cut into 8 pieces (2 legs, 2 thighs, 2 breasts, 2 wings)
1 to 1½ cups pork lard, vegetable oil, or peanut oil
1. In a large bowl, combine all the dry ingredients. Mix together with a fork until thoroughly combined. Set aside.
2. In another large bowl, beat the eggs into the buttermilk. Coat the chicken pieces in the egg-and-buttermilk mixture, and then dredge them in the seasoned flour. Repeat, coating the chicken again with the egg-and-buttermilk mixture and then dredging them again in the seasoned flour mixture, to create a double layer of batter. Set the pieces on a clean platter.
3. Pour the lard or oil to a depth of 1 inch in a large cast-iron skillet, and heat it over medium heat until the temperature reaches 325ºF (163ºC) on a deep-frying thermometer. Add the chicken pieces, in batches, and cook for about 20 minutes, turning them over halfway through cooking. The wings will be done after 10 minutes. Drain the chicken thoroughly on paper towels, and serve immediately.

Beer Chicken with Butter

Prep time: 30 minutes | Cook time: 3 to 4 hours | Serves 3 to 4

8 tablespoons (1 stick) unsalted butter, melted

½ cup apple cider vinegar

½ cup Cajun seasoning, divided

1 teaspoon garlic powder

1 teaspoon onion powder

1 (4-pound / 1.8-kg) whole chicken, giblets removed

Extra-virgin olive oil, for rubbing

1 (12-ounce / 340-g) can beer

1 cup apple juice

½ cup extra-virgin olive oil

1. In a small bowl, whisk together the butter, vinegar, ¼ cup of Cajun seasoning, garlic powder, and onion powder.

2. Use a meat-injecting syringe to inject the liquid into various spots in the chicken. Inject about half of the mixture into the breasts and the other half throughout the rest of the chicken.

3. Rub the chicken all over with olive oil and apply the remaining ¼ cup of Cajun seasoning, being sure to rub under the skin as well.

4. Drink or discard half the beer and place the opened beer can on a stable surface.

5. Place the bird's cavity on top of the can and position the chicken so it will sit up by itself. Prop the legs forward to make the bird more stable, or buy an inexpensive, specially made stand to hold the beer can and chicken in place.

6. Supply your smoker with wood pellets and follow the manufacturer's specific start-up procedure. Preheat, with the lid closed, to 250ºF (121ºC).

7. In a clean spray bottle, combine the apple juice and olive oil. Cover and shake the mop sauce well before each use.

8. Carefully put the chicken on the grill. Close the lid and smoke the chicken for 3 to 4 hours, spraying with the mop sauce every hour, until golden brown and a meat thermometer inserted in the thickest part of the thigh reads 165ºF (74ºC). Keep a piece of aluminum foil handy to loosely cover the chicken if the skin begins to brown too quickly.

9. Let the meat rest for 5 minutes before carving.

Chicken Cheese Buffalo Wraps

Prep time: 30 minutes | Cook time: 20 minutes | Serves 4

2 teaspoons poultry seasoning

1 teaspoon freshly ground black pepper

1 teaspoon garlic powder

1 to 1½ pounds (454 to 680 g) chicken tenders

4 tablespoons (½ stick) unsalted butter, melted

½ cup hot sauce (such as Frank's RedHot)

4 (10-inch) flour tortillas

1 cup shredded lettuce

½ cup diced tomato

½ cup diced celery

½ cup diced red onion

½ cup shredded Cheddar cheese

¼ cup blue cheese crumbles

¼ cup prepared ranch dressing

2 tablespoons sliced pickled jalapeño peppers (optional)

1. Supply your smoker with wood pellets and follow the manufacturer's specific start-up procedure. Preheat, with the lid closed, to 350ºF (177ºC).

2. In a small bowl, stir together the poultry seasoning, pepper, and garlic powder to create an all-purpose rub, and season the chicken tenders with it.

3. Arrange the tenders directly on the grill, close the lid, and smoke for 20 minutes, or until a meat thermometer inserted in the thickest part of the meat reads 170ºF (77ºC).

4. In another bowl, stir together the melted butter and hot sauce and coat the smoked chicken with it.

5. To serve, heat the tortillas on the grill for less than a minute on each side and place on a plate.

6. Top each tortilla with some of the lettuce, tomato, celery, red onion, Cheddar cheese, blue cheese crumbles, ranch dressing, and jalapeños (if using).

7. Divide the chicken among the tortillas, close up securely, and serve.

Chicken with Rub

Prep time: 15 minutes | Cook time: 1 to 2 hours | Serves 6 to 8

1 whole chicken

2 tablespoons olive oil

1 batch Chicken Rub

1. Supply your smoker with wood pellets and follow the manufacturer's specific start-up procedure. Preheat the grill, with the lid closed, to 375ºF (191ºC).

2. Coat the chicken all over with olive oil and season it with the rub. Using your hands, work the rub into the meat.

3. Place the chicken directly on the grill grate and smoke until its internal temperature reaches 170ºF (77ºC).

4. Remove the chicken from the grill and let it rest for 10 minutes, before carving and serving.

Chicken Breasts

Prep time: 15 minutes | Cook time: 1 hour 25 minutes | Serves 4 to 6

2½ pounds (1.1 kg) boneless, skinless chicken breasts

Salt and freshly ground black pepper, to taste

1. Supply your smoker with wood pellets and follow the manufacturer's specific start-up procedure. Preheat the grill, with the lid closed, to 180ºF (82ºC).

2. Season the chicken breasts all over with salt and pepper.

3. Place the breasts directly on the grill grate and smoke for 1 hour.

4. Increase the grill's temperature to 325ºF (163ºC) and continue to cook until the chicken's internal temperature reaches 170ºF (77ºC). Remove the breasts from the grill and serve immediately.

Rubbed Chicken Breast

Prep time: 10 minutes | Cook time: 45 minutes | Serves 2 to 4

2 (1-pound / 454-g) bone-in, skin-on chicken breast

1 batch Chicken Rub

1. Supply your smoker with wood pellets and follow the manufacturer's specific start-up procedure. Preheat the grill, with the lid closed, to 350ºF (177ºC).

2. Season the chicken breast all over with the rub. Using your hands, work the rub into the meat.

3. Place the chicken breast directly on the grill grate and smoke until their internal temperature reaches 170ºF (77ºC). Remove the breasts from the grill and serve immediately.

Chicken Breast Tenders

Prep time: 15 minutes | Cook time: 1 hour 20 minutes | Serves 2 to 4

1 pound (454 g) boneless, skinless chicken breast tenders

1 batch Chicken Rub

1. Supply your smoker with wood pellets and follow the manufacturer's specific start-up procedure. Preheat the grill, with the lid closed, to 180ºF (82ºC).

2. Season the chicken tenders with the rub. Using your hands, work the rub into the meat.

3. Place the tenders directly on the grill grate and smoke for 1 hour.

4. Increase the grill's temperature to 300ºF (149ºC) and continue to cook until the tenders' internal temperature reaches 170ºF (77ºC). Remove the tenders from the grill and serve immediately.

Chicken Wings with Hot Sauce

Prep time: 15 minutes | Cook time: 35 minutes | Serves 2 to 3

1 pound (454 g) chicken wings

1 batch Chicken Rub

1 cup Frank's Red-Hot Sauce, Buffalo wing sauce, or similar

1. Supply your smoker with wood pellets and follow the manufacturer's specific start-up procedure. Preheat the grill, with the lid closed, to 300ºF (149ºC).

2. Season the chicken wings with the rub. Using your hands, work the rub into the meat.

3. Place the wings directly on the grill grate and smoke until their internal temperature reaches 160ºF (71ºC).

4. Baste the wings with the sauce and continue to smoke until the wings' internal temperature reaches 170ºF (77ºC).

Chicken Wings with BBQ Sauce

Prep time: 20 minutes | Cook time: 1 hour 25 minutes | Serves 2 to 4

1 pound (454 g) chicken wings

1 batch Sweet and Spicy Rub

1 cup barbecue sauce

1. Supply your smoker with wood pellets and follow the manufacturer's specific start-up procedure. Preheat the grill, with the lid closed, to 325ºF (163ºC).

2. Season the chicken wings with the rub. Using your hands, work the rub into the meat.

3. Place the wings directly on the grill grate and cook until they reach an internal temperature of 165ºF (74ºC).

4. Transfer the wings into an aluminum pan. Add the barbecue sauce and stir to coat the wings.

5. Reduce the grill's temperature to 250ºF (121ºC) and put the pan on the grill. Smoke the wings for 1 hour more, uncovered. Remove the wings from the grill and serve immediately.

Chicken Drumsticks

Prep time: 15 minutes | Cook time: 25 minutes | Serves 2 to 4

1 pound (454 g) chicken drumsticks

2 tablespoons olive oil

1 batch Sweet and Spicy Rub

1. Supply your smoker with wood pellets and follow the manufacturer's specific start-up procedure. Preheat the grill, with the lid closed, to 350ºF (177ºC).

2. Coat the drumsticks all over with olive oil and season with the rub. Using your hands, work the rub into the meat.

3. Place the drumsticks directly on the grill grate and smoke until their internal temperature reaches 170ºF (77ºC). Remove the drumsticks from the grill and serve immediately.

Chicken Quarters with Butter

Prep time: 15 minutes | Cook time: 2 hours | Serves 2 to 4

4 chicken quarters

2 tablespoons olive oil

1 batch Chicken Rub

2 tablespoons butter

1. Supply your smoker with wood pellets and follow the manufacturer's specific start-up procedure. Preheat the grill, with the lid closed, to 180ºF (82ºC).

2. Coat the chicken quarters all over with olive oil and season them with the rub. Using your hands, work the rub into the meat.

3. Place the quarters directly on the grill grate and smoke for 1½ hours.

4. Baste the quarters with the butter and increase the grill's temperature to 375ºF (191ºC). Continue to cook until the chicken's internal temperature reaches 170ºF (77ºC).

5. Remove the quarters from the grill and let them rest for 10 minutes before serving.

Lemony Chicken

Prep time: 10 minutes | Cook time: 1 to 2 hours | Serves 4

1 (4-pound / 1.8-kg) whole chicken, giblets removed

Extra-virgin olive oil, for rubbing

3 tablespoons Greek seasoning

Juice of 1 lemon

Butcher's string

1. Supply your smoker with wood pellets and follow the manufacturer's specific start-up procedure. Preheat, with the lid closed, to 450ºF (232ºC).

2. Rub the bird generously all over with oil, including inside the cavity.

3. Sprinkle the Greek seasoning all over and under the skin of the bird, and squeeze the lemon juice over the breast.

4. Tuck the chicken wings behind the back and tie the legs together with butcher's string or cooking twine.

5. Put the chicken directly on the grill, breast-side up, close the lid, and roast for 1 hour to 1 hour 30 minutes, or until a meat thermometer inserted in the thigh reads 165ºF (74ºC).

6. Let the meat rest for 10 minutes before carving.

Chiles Chicken Cheese Enchiladas

Prep time: 15 minutes | Cook time: 45 minutes | Serves 6

6 cups diced cooked chicken

3 cups grated Monterey Jack cheese, divided

1 cup sour cream

1 (4-ounce / 113-g) can chopped green chiles

2 (10-ounce / 284-g) cans red or green enchilada sauce, divided

12 (8-inch) flour tortillas

½ cup chopped scallions

¼ cup chopped fresh cilantro

1. Supply your smoker with wood pellets and follow the manufacturer's specific start-up procedure. Preheat, with the lid closed, to 350ºF (177ºC).

2. In a large bowl, combine the cooked chicken, 2 cups of cheese, the sour cream, and green chiles to make the filling.

3. Pour one can of enchilada sauce in the bottom of a 9-by-13-inch baking dish or aluminum pan.

4. Spoon ⅓ cup of the filling on each tortilla and roll up securely.

5. Transfer the tortillas seam-side down to the baking dish, then pour the remaining can of enchilada sauce over them, coating all exposed surfaces of the tortillas.

6. Sprinkle the remaining 1 cup of cheese over the enchiladas and cover tightly with aluminum foil.

7. Bake on the grill, with the lid closed, for 30 minutes, then remove the foil.

8. Continue baking with the lid closed for 15 minutes, or until bubbly.

9. Garnish the enchiladas with the chopped scallions and cilantro and serve immediately.

Roast Chicken Thighs

Prep time: 5 minutes | Cook time: 1 to 2 hours | Serves 12 to 15

3 pounds (1.4 kg) chicken thighs

2 teaspoons salt

2 teaspoons freshly ground black pepper

2 teaspoons garlic powder

2 teaspoons onion powder

2 cups prepared Italian dressing

1. Place the chicken thighs in a shallow dish and sprinkle with the salt, pepper, garlic powder, and onion powder, being sure to get under the skin.

2. Cover with the Italian dressing, coating all sides, and refrigerate for 1 hour.

3. Supply your smoker with wood pellets and follow the manufacturer's specific start-up procedure. Preheat, with the lid closed, to 250ºF (121ºC).

4. Remove the chicken thighs from the marinade and place directly on the grill, skin-side down. Discard the marinade.

5. Close the lid and roast the chicken for 1 hour 30 minutes to 2 hours, or until a meat thermometer inserted in the thickest part of the thighs reads 165ºF (74ºC). Do not turn the thighs during the smoking process.

Chicken with Butter

Prep time: 30 minutes | Cook time: 55 minutes | Serves 4 to 6

1 egg, beaten

½ cup milk

1 cup all-purpose flour

2 tablespoons salt

1 tablespoon freshly ground black pepper

2 teaspoons freshly ground white pepper

2 teaspoons cayenne pepper

2 teaspoons garlic powder

2 teaspoons onion powder

1 teaspoon smoked paprika

8 tablespoons (1 stick) unsalted butter, melted

1 whole chicken, cut up into pieces

1. Supply your smoker with wood pellets and follow the manufacturer's specific start-up procedure. Preheat, with the lid closed, to 375ºF (191ºC).

2. In a medium bowl, combine the beaten egg with the milk and set aside.

3. In a separate medium bowl, stir together the flour, salt, black pepper, white pepper, cayenne, garlic powder, onion powder, and smoked paprika.

4. Line the bottom and sides of a high-sided metal baking pan with aluminum foil to ease cleanup.

5. Pour the melted butter into the prepared pan.

6. Dip the chicken pieces one at a time in the egg mixture, and then coat well with the seasoned flour. Transfer to the baking pan.

7. Smoke the chicken in the pan of butter ("smo-fry") on the grill, with the lid closed, for 25 minutes, then reduce the heat to 325°F (163°C) and turn the chicken pieces over.

8. Continue smoking with the lid closed for about 30 minutes, or until a meat thermometer inserted in the thickest part of each chicken piece reads 165°F (74°C).

9. Serve immediately.

Chicken with Teriyaki Sauce

Prep time: 20 minutes | Cook time: 1 to 2 hours | Serves 4

2 boneless chicken breasts with drumettes attached

½ cup soy sauce

½ cup teriyaki sauce

¼ cup canola oil

¼ cup white vinegar

1 tablespoon minced garlic

¼ cup chopped scallions

2 teaspoons freshly ground black pepper

1 teaspoon ground mustard

1. Place the chicken in a baking dish.

2. In a bowl, whisk together the soy sauce, teriyaki sauce, canola oil, vinegar, garlic, scallions, pepper and ground mustard, then pour this marinade over the chicken, coating both sides.

3. Refrigerate the chicken in marinade for 4 hours, turning over every hour.

4. When ready to smoke the chicken, supply your smoker with wood pellets and follow the manufacturer's specific start-up procedure. Preheat, with the lid closed, to 250°F (121°C).

5. Remove the chicken from the marinade but do not rinse. Discard the marinade.

6. Arrange the chicken directly on the grill, close the lid, and smoke for 1 hour 30 minutes to 2 hours, or until a meat thermometer inserted in the thickest part of the meat reads 165°F (74°C).

7. Let the meat rest for 3 minutes before serving.

Chicken with BBQ Sauce

Prep time: 10 minutes | Cook time: 1 to 2 hours | Serves 8

8 boneless, skinless chicken breasts

2 teaspoons salt

2 teaspoons freshly ground black pepper

2 teaspoons garlic powder

2 cups Molasses BBQ Sauce or your preferred barbecue sauce, divided

1. Supply your smoker with wood pellets and follow the manufacturer's specific start-up procedure. Preheat, with the lid closed, to 250°F (121°C).

2. Place the chicken breasts in a large pan and sprinkle both sides with the salt, pepper, and garlic powder, being sure to rub under the skin.

3. Place the roasting pan on the grill, close the lid, and smoke for 1 hour 30 minutes to 2 hours, or until a meat thermometer inserted in the thickest part of each breast reads 165°F (74°C). During the last 15 minutes of cooking, cover the chicken with 1 cup of barbecue sauce.

4. Serve the chicken warm with the remaining 1 cup of barbecue sauce.

Chicken with Ranch Dressing

Prep time: 10 minutes | Cook time: 1 hour | Serves 4

2 pounds (907 g) chicken wings

2 tablespoons extra-virgin olive oil

2 packages ranch dressing mix (such as Hidden Valley brand)

¼ cup prepared ranch dressing (optional)

1.   Supply your smoker with wood pellets and follow the manufacturer's specific start-up procedure. Preheat, with the lid closed, to 350ºF (177ºC).

2.   Place the chicken wings in a large bowl and toss with the olive oil and ranch dressing mix.

3.   Arrange the wings directly on the grill, or line the grill with aluminum foil for easy cleanup, close the lid, and smoke for 25 minutes.

4.   Flip and smoke for 20 to 35 minutes more, or until a meat thermometer inserted in the thickest part of the wings reads 165ºF (74ºC) and the wings are crispy.

5.   Serve warm with ranch dressing (if using).

Spinach Hasselback Cheese Chicken

Prep time: 25 minutes | Cook time: 25 to 30 minutes | Serves 4

Brine:

¼ cup salt

¼ cup packed light brown sugar

6 cups water

4 boneless, skinless chicken breasts

Stuffing and Chicken:

1 cup grated Asiago cheese

1 cup torn fresh spinach leaves

8 ounces (227 g) cream cheese, softened

1 tablespoon minced garlic

2 teaspoons salt

1 tablespoon plus 1 teaspoon freshly ground black pepper, divided

2 teaspoons poultry seasoning

2 teaspoons garlic powder

2 teaspoons onion powder

Make the Brine

1.   In a large bowl, combine the salt and brown sugar with 6 cups of water, stirring to dissolve.

2.   Add the chicken breasts to the brine, cover, and refrigerate for 2 hours.

3.   Remove the chicken from the brine, rinse it, and discard the brine.

Make the Stuffing and Chicken

4.   Supply your smoker with wood pellets and follow the manufacturer's specific start-up procedure. Preheat, with the lid closed, to 350ºF (177ºC).

5.   In a bowl, stir together the Asiago cheese, spinach leaves, cream cheese, minced garlic, salt, and 2 teaspoons of pepper; set aside.

6.   Cut parallel lines horizontally down the length of each chicken breast to create the "Hasselback" style: deep cuts, but not all the way through the chicken.

7.   In another bowl, mix together the poultry seasoning, remaining 2 teaspoons of pepper, the garlic powder, and onion powder to form a rub, and season the chicken well with it.

8.   Slather the spinach-cream cheese mixture inside each incision in the breasts, using up all of the mixture.

9.   Place the chicken breasts in a cast iron skillet on the grill, close the lid, and smoke for 25 to 30 minutes, or until the juices run clear and a meat thermometer inserted in the thickest part of the meat reads 170ºF (77ºC).

Bacon and Ham Cheese Chicken

Prep time: 30 minutes | Cook time: 2 to 2½ hours | Serves 6

24 bacon slices

3 large boneless, skinless chicken breasts, butterflied

3 tablespoons roasted garlic–flavored extra-virgin olive oil

3 tablespoons Sweet Dry Rub with Paprika or Poultry Seasoning

12 slices black forest ham

12 slices provolone cheese

1. Tightly weave 4 slices of bacon together, leaving extra space on the ends. The bacon weave interlocks alternate slices of bacon and is used to wrap around the chicken cordon bleu.

2. Spritz or rub 2 thin chicken breast fillets with the olive oil on both sides.

3. Dust both sides of the chicken breast fillets with the seasoning.

4. Layer one seasoned chicken fillet on the bacon weave and top with 1 slice each of ham and provolone cheese.

5. Repeat the process with another chicken fillet, ham, and cheese. Fold the chicken, ham, and cheese in half.

6. Overlap the bacon strips from opposite corners to completely cover the chicken cordon blue.

7. Use silicone food-grade cooking bands, butcher's twine, or toothpicks to secure the bacon strips in place.

8. Repeat the process for the remaining chicken breasts and ingredients.

9. Configure your wood pellet smoker-grill for indirect cooking and preheat for smoking, 180ºF (82ºC) to 200ºF (93ºC), using apple or cherry pellets.

10. Smoke the bacon cordon bleu for 1 hour.

11. After smoking for an hour, increase the pit temperature to 350ºF (177ºC).

12. The bacon cordon bleu is done when the internal temperature reaches 165ºF (74ºC) and the bacon is crisp.

13. Rest under a loose foil tent for 15 minutes before serving.

Chicken Drumsticks with Teriyaki

Prep time: 15 minutes | Cook time: 1½ to 2 hours | Serves 4

3 cups teriyaki marinade and cooking sauce, like Mr. Yoshida's Original Gourmet

3 teaspoons Poultry Seasoning

1 teaspoon garlic powder

10 chicken drumsticks

1. In a medium bowl, mix the marinade and cooking sauce with the Poultry Seasoning and garlic powder.

2. Peel back the skin on the drumsticks to facilitate marinade penetration.

3. Place the drumsticks in a marinating pan or 1-gallon plastic sealable bag, and pour the marinade mixture over the drumsticks. Refrigerate overnight.

4. Rotate the chicken drumsticks in the morning.

5. Configure your wood pellet-smoker grill for indirect cooking.

6. Replace the skin over the drumsticks, and hang the drumsticks on a poultry leg-and-wing rack to drain on a cooking sheet on your counter while the grill is preheating. If you don't own a poultry leg-and-wing rack you can lightly pat the drumsticks dry with paper towels.

7. Preheat your wood pellet smoker-grill to 180ºF (82ºC) using hickory or maple pellets.

8. Smoke the marinated chicken drumsticks for 1 hour.

9. After an hour, increase the pit temperature to 350ºF (177ºC) and cook the drumsticks for an additional 30 to 45 minutes, until the thickest part of the drumsticks reach an internal temperature of 180ºF (82ºC).

10. Rest the chicken drumsticks under a loose foil tent for 15 minutes before serving.

Grilled Chicken Quarters

Prep time: 20 minutes | Cook time: 1 to 1½ hours | Serves 4

4 fresh or thawed frozen chicken quarters

4 to 6 tablespoons extra-virgin olive oil

4 tablespoons Sweet Dry Rub with Paprika

1. Trim the chicken quarters of any excess skin and fat. Carefully peel back the chicken skin and rub the olive oil on and under the skin of each chicken quarter.

2. Season on and under the skins and on the backs of the chicken quarters with Sweet Dry Rub with Paprika.

3. Wrap the seasoned chicken quarters in plastic wrap and refrigerate for 2 to 4 hours to give the flavors time to absorb.

4. Configure your wood pellet smoker-grill for indirect cooking and preheat to 325ºF (163ºC) using any pellets.

5. Place the chicken quarters on the grill and cook for 1 hour at 325ºF (163ºC).

6. After an hour, increase the pit temperature to 400ºF (204ºC) to finish the chicken quarters and crisp the skins.

7. Pull the crispy chicken quarters off the grill when the internal temperature, at the thickest parts of the thighs and legs, reaches 180ºF (82ºC) and the juices run clear.

8. Rest the grilled crispy chicken quarters under a loose foil tent for 15 minutes before serving.

Hens with Lemon

Prep time: 15 minutes | Cook time: 1 hour 45 minutes | Serves 4

4 cups vegetable broth

4 cups cold water

1 tablespoon whole black peppercorns

¼ cup brown sugar

1 cup kosher salt

4 Cornish game hens

2 lemons

2 medium oranges

2 tablespoons ground coriander

1 teaspoon ginger

1 teaspoon cumin

¼ cup olive oil

Salt and pepper, to taste

1. To make the brine, bring the vegetable broth, water, black peppercorns, sugar and salt to a boil in a large pot, stirring until the salt is dissolved. Remove the brine from the heat and set aside to cool. When the brine is cool, place the Cornish hens in the brine and refrigerate for 2 to 3 hours. Do not overbrine or the hens will get too salty.

2. Prepare your Traeger by turning it to the SMOKE setting. Wait about 5 minutes for it to produce smoke, then set the Traeger to run at 350ºF (177ºC).

3. Remove the hens from the brine, and pat dry. Discard the brine.

4. Cut the lemons and oranges into quarters and place in a microwave-safe bowl and sprinkle with the coriander, ginger and cumin. Microwave on high for 2 minutes. Using a spoon

or tongs, stuff the mixture into the cavities of the Cornish hens. Brush each hen with the olive oil and sprinkle with salt and pepper. Place the stuffed hens into a disposable aluminum half-size tray, breast sides up.

5.   Roast the hens for about 1 hour and 45 minutes or until an instant-read thermometer inserted into the thickest part of the thigh near the bone reads 180ºF (82ºC).

6.   For crispier skin, increase the heat to 400ºF (204ºC) for the last 15 minutes of cooking.

7.   Rest the hens for 10 minutes before serving. Resting the meat before serving helps to prevent the juices from running out when sliced.

Beer Chicken with Mayo

Prep time: 10 minutes | Cook time: 3 hours | Serves 4 to 6

1 (12-ounce / 340-g) can of your favorite beer
1 (4-pound / 1.8-kg) whole chicken
½ cup mayonnaise
⅓ cup your favorite BBQ rub

1.   Open the can of beer and discard half.

2.   Lower the cavity of the chicken over the top of the can with the legs supporting some of the weight. Arrange the chicken in a half-size disposable aluminum pan so that the can is holding up the chicken with legs pointed downward. We prefer to cook in an aluminum pan for two reasons. One is that it will better support the weight of the chicken. Second, it will catch and retain the drippings, which keeps the smoker clean and lets the fire burn pure.

3.   In a small bowl, combine the mayonnaise and rub and mix thoroughly. Pat the chicken dry and then, using your hands, rub the mixture all over the bird. Don't be bashful—more is better here.

4.   Prepare your Traeger by turning it to the SMOKE setting. Wait about 5 minutes for it to produce smoke, then set the Traeger to run at 225ºF (107ºC).

5.   Place your beer can chicken in the pan on the Traeger and cook for 1 hour. After 1 hour, increase the temperature to 300ºF (149ºC) and cook for 2 hours, or until the internal temperature of the meat in the breast reaches 165ºF (74ºC). I recommend cooking this way as the lower heat produces more smoke so cooking in two stages allows you to get a great smoke flavor and a perfectly cooked chicken.

6.   Remove the pan from the Traeger, tent with some foil and let the chicken rest for 15 minutes before slicing.

Chicken Breast with Garlic

Prep time: 15 minutes | Cook time: 20 minutes | Serves 6

6 thick chicken breasts, boneless and skinless
Brine:
½ cup brown sugar
½ cup kosher salt
1 quart room-temperature water
2 tablespoons whole peppercorns
2 cloves garlic, crushed
Rub:
2 teaspoons kosher salt
1 teaspoon ground black pepper
1 teaspoon garlic powder
1 teaspoon smoked paprika
½ teaspoon coriander
½ teaspoon cumin
2 tablespoons olive oil

1.   To make the brine, dissolve the brown sugar and salt in the water in a large pot. Add the peppercorns and crushed garlic. Add the chicken,

making sure the chicken is completely submerged in brine mixture. Place the pot in the refrigerator for 2 hours. Make sure not to leave the chicken in the brine any longer than 2 hours—doing so can lead to an overly salty end product. Remove the chicken from the pot, rinse and pat dry.

2. Set your Traeger to HIGH and close the lid for 15 minutes to preheat.

3. While your Traeger is preheating, make the rub. Combine the salt, black pepper, garlic powder, paprika, coriander and cumin in a small bowl.

4. Coat the chicken lightly with the olive oil, making sure to cover all sides. Sprinkle the chicken liberally with rub on all sides. Place the chicken directly on the grates of the preheated Traeger and cook on each side 5 to 8 minutes or until the internal temperature reaches 165ºF (74ºC). Let rest for 10 minutes before serving.

Chicken with Sesame Ginger Sauce

Prep time: 25 minutes | Cook time: 45 to 60 minutes | Makes 24 pieces

24 jumbo party wings (about 3 pounds / 1.4 kg)

Rub:

2 tablespoons baking powder

1 tablespoon ground ginger

1 teaspoon salt

1 teaspoon onion powder

1 teaspoon garlic powder

½ teaspoon cayenne pepper

Sesame Ginger Sauce:

⅓ cup soy sauce

⅓ cup sweet rice wine

⅓ cup water

1 tablespoon sesame oil

2 teaspoons Sriracha

1 tablespoon ground ginger

2 cloves garlic, minced

1 tablespoon cornstarch

Salt and pepper, to taste

3 tablespoons water

½ cup sugar

1. Preheat the Traeger to 375ºF (191ºC).

2. To make the rub, in a medium bowl, mix the baking powder, ground ginger, salt, onion powder, garlic powder and cayenne pepper together. Add half of the rub to a large resealable plastic bag. Add half of the wings and shake until coated evenly. Remove the wings from the bag and put them on a tray; make sure none of them are touching. Add the remaining rub and wings to the plastic bag and repeat the process.

3. Place the wings on the grill and watch closely so the wings do not burn. Flip the wings after 30 minutes and grill the other side until crispy, 15 to 30 minutes more.

4. To make the sesame ginger sauce, in a medium bowl, whisk together the soy sauce, sweet rice wine, water, sesame oil, Sriracha, ginger, garlic, cornstarch, salt and pepper. Set aside. Add the water and sugar to a medium skillet and boil over medium heat for 1 minute. Do not overcook. Add the soy sauce mixture and simmer until thickened, about 2 minutes. Remove the sauce from the heat and allow to cool slightly. Add the cooked chicken to a large bowl, then add the sauce. Toss until the wings are evenly coated.

Thyme Chicken Breast with Lemon

Prep time: 15 minutes | Cook time: 15 minutes | Serves 6

6 chicken breasts, skinless and boneless

½ cup oil

1 to 2 fresh thyme sprigs

1 teaspoon. ground black pepper

2 teaspoons salt

2 teaspoons honey

1 garlic clove, chopped

1 lemon the juice and zest

lemon wedges, for serving

1.   Make the marinade: In a bowl combine the thyme, black pepper, salt, honey, garlic, and lemon zest and juice. Stir until dissolved and combined. Add in the oil and whisk to combine.

2.   Clean the breasts and pat dry. Place them in a plastic bag. Pour the pre-made marinade and massage to distribute evenly. Place in the fridge, 4 hours.

3.   Preheat the grill to 400ºF (204ºC) with the lid closed.

4.   Drain the chicken and grill until the internal temperature reaches 165ºF (74ºC), about 15 minutes.

5.   Serve with lemon wedges and a side dish of your choice.

Chicken Burgers with Onion

Prep time: 20 minutes | Cook time: 1 hour 10 minutes | Serves 6

2 pounds (907 g) ground chicken breast

⅔ cup finely chopped onions

1 tablespoon cilantro, finely chopped

2 tablespoons fresh parsley, finely chopped

2 tablespoons olive oil

½ teaspoon ground cumin

2 tablespoons lemon juice freshly squeezed

¾ teaspoon salt and red pepper

1.   In a bowl add all ingredients; mix until combined well.

2.   Form the mixture into 6 patties.

3.   Start your pellet grill on SMOKE (oak or apple pellets) with the lid open until the fire is established. Set the temperature to 350ºF (177ºC) and preheat, lid closed, for 10 to 15 minutes.

4.   Smoke the chicken burgers for 45 to 50 minutes or until cooked through, turning every 15 minutes.

5.   Your burgers are ready when internal temperature reaches 165ºF (74ºC).

6.   Serve hot.

Chicken Patties

Prep time: 20 minutes | Cook time: 50 minutes | Serves 6

2 pounds (907 g) ground chicken breast

⅔ cup minced onion

1 tablespoon cilantro, chopped

2 tablespoons fresh parsley, finely chopped

2 tablespoons olive oil

⅛ teaspoon crushed red pepper flakes, or to taste

½ teaspoon ground cumin

2 tablespoons fresh lemon juice

¾ teaspoon kosher salt

2 teaspoons paprika

Hamburger buns, for serving

1.   In a bowl combine all ingredients from the list.

2.   Using your hands, mix well. Form mixture into 6 patties. Refrigerate until ready to grill (about 30 minutes).

3.   Start your pellet grill on SMOKE with the lid open until the fire is established). Set the temperature to 350ºF (177ºC) and preheat, lid closed, for 10 to 15 minutes.

4.   Arrange chicken patties on the grill rack and cook for 35 to 40 minutes turning once.

5.   Serve hot with hamburger buns and your favorite condiments.

Chicken Breasts with Sage

Prep time: 15 minutes | Cook time: 40 minutes | Serves 4

4 chicken breasts boneless

¼ cup garlic-infused olive oil

2 clove garlic minced

¼ teaspoon dried sage

¼ teaspoon dried lavender

¼ teaspoon dried thyme

¼ teaspoon dried mint

½ tablespoon dried crushed red pepper

Kosher salt, to taste

1.   Place the chicken breasts in a shallow plastic container.

2.   In a bowl, combine all remaining ingredients, and pour the mixture over the chicken breast and refrigerate for one hour.

3.   Remove the chicken breast from the sauce (reserve sauce) and pat dry on kitchen paper.

4.   Start your pellet grill on SMOKE (hickory pellet) with the lid open until the fire is established). Set the temperature to 250ºF (121ºC) and preheat, lid closed, for 10 to 15 minutes.

5.   Place chicken breasts on the smoker. Close pellet grill lid and cook for about 30 to 40 minutes or until chicken breasts reach 165ºF (74ºC).

6.   Serve hot with reserved marinade.

Chili Chicken with Honey

Prep time: 10 minutes | Cook time: 1 hour 15 minutes | Serves 6

2 pounds (907 g) chicken tenders

1 cup sweet chili sauce

¼ cup fresh pineapple juice

¼ cup honey

1.   Combine the honey, pineapple juice, and sweet chili sauce in a medium bowl. Whisk together thoroughly.

2.   Put ¼ cup of the mixture to one side.

3.   Coat the chicken in the sauce.

4.   Place a lid over the bowl and leave it in the fridge for 30 minutes to marinate.

5.   Heat the grill to high heat.

6.   Separate the chicken from the marinade and grill for 5 minutes on each side.

7.   Use the reserved sauce to brush over the chicken.

8.   Continue to grill for a further 1 minute on each side.

9.   Take the chicken off the grill and let it rest for 5 minutes before servings.

Tangy Chicken

Prep time: 15 minutes | Cook time: 45 minutes | Serves 4

1 whole chicken, backbone removed (3 to 4 pounds / 1.4 to 1.8 kg)

2 oranges

¼ cup oil

2 teaspoons Dijon mustard

1 orange, zest

2 tablespoons rosemary leaves, chopped

2 teaspoons salt

1. Clean and pat your chicken dry.

2. Take a bowl and mix in orange juice, oil, orange zest, salt, rosemary leaves, Dijon mustard and mix well.

3. Marinade chicken for 2 hours or overnight.

4. Preheat your grill to 350ºF (177ºC).

5. Transfer your chicken to the smoker and smoke for 30 minutes skin down. Flip and smoke until the internal temperature reaches 175ºF (79ºC) in the thigh and 165ºF (74ºC) in the breast.

6. Let it rest for 10 minutes and carve.

7. Enjoy!

CHAPTER 7: TURKEY

Turkey with Garlic

Prep time: 15 minutes | Cook time: 5 hours | Serves 10 to 12

1 (12- to 15-pound /5.4- to 6.8-kg) turkey, neck and giblets removed

8 cups chicken broth

3 medium white onions, diced

4 cloves garlic, crushed

1 cup (packed) dark brown sugar

2 cups Jack's Old South Huney Muney Cluck Rub, or 1 recipe Chili Chicken Rub

1. Rinse the turkey inside and out, and pat it dry thoroughly. Place the turkey in a large roasting bag, and add the chicken broth, onions, garlic, and brown sugar. Tie the bag to seal it and place it in a large roasting pan. Allow the turkey to marinate this way in the refrigerator overnight.

2. When you are ready to cook the turkey, heat a smoker to 250ºF (121ºC).

3. Remove the turkey from the bag, and discard the marinade. Apply the rub all over the bird. Put the turkey on a rack in a large, deep aluminum pan, place the pan in the smoker, and cook for 5 hours or until the breast meat reaches an internal temperature of 165ºF (74ºC).

4. Remove the pan from the smoker. Allow the turkey to rest, loosely covered with foil, for 30 minutes. Then carve the turkey, and serve immediately.

Turkey Duck and Chicken Roulade

Prep time: 20 minutes | Cook time: 2 hours | Serves 6

1 (16-ounce / 454-g) boneless turkey breast

1 (8- to 10-ounce / 227- to 284-g) boneless duck breast

1 (8-ounce / 227-g) boneless, skinless chicken breast

Salt and freshly ground black pepper, to taste

2 cups Italian dressing

2 tablespoons Cajun seasoning

1 cup prepared seasoned stuffing mix

8 slices bacon

Butcher's string

1. Butterfly the turkey, duck, and chicken breasts, cover with plastic wrap and, using a mallet, flatten each ½ inch thick.

2. Season all the meat on both sides with a little salt and pepper.

3. In a medium bowl, combine the Italian dressing and Cajun seasoning. Spread one-fourth of the mixture on top of the flattened turkey breast.

4. Place the duck breast on top of the turkey, spread it with one-fourth of the dressing mixture, and top with the stuffing mix.

5. Place the chicken breast on top of the duck and spread with one-fourth of the dressing mixture.

6. Supply your smoker with wood pellets and follow the manufacturer's specific start-up procedure. Preheat, with the lid closed, to 275ºF (135ºC).

7. Tightly roll up the stack, tie with butcher's string, and slather the whole thing with the remaining dressing mixture.

8. Wrap the bacon slices around the turducken and secure with toothpicks, or try making a bacon weave (see the technique for this in the Jalapeño-Bacon Pork Tenderloin recipe).

9. Place the turducken roulade in a roasting pan. Transfer to the grill, close the lid, and roast for 2 hours, or until a meat thermometer inserted in the turducken reads 165ºF (74ºC). Tent with aluminum foil in the last 30 minutes, if necessary, to keep from overbrowning.

10. Let the turducken rest for 15 to 20 minutes before carving. Serve warm.

Buttery Turkey

Prep time: 10 minutes | Cook time: 5 to 6 hours | Serves 6 to 8

1 (10- to 12-pound / 4.5- to 5.4-kg) turkey, giblets removed
Extra-virgin olive oil, for rubbing
¼ cup poultry seasoning
8 tablespoons (1 stick) unsalted butter, melted
½ cup apple juice
2 teaspoons dried sage
2 teaspoons dried thyme

1. Supply your smoker with wood pellets and follow the manufacturer's specific start-up procedure. Preheat, with the lid closed, to 250ºF (121ºC).

2. Rub the turkey with oil and season with the poultry seasoning inside and out, getting under the skin.

3. In a bowl, combine the melted butter, apple juice, sage, and thyme to use for basting.

4. Put the turkey in a roasting pan, place on the grill, close the lid, and grill for 5 to 6 hours, basting every hour, until the skin is brown and crispy, or until a meat thermometer inserted in the thickest part of the thigh reads 165ºF (74ºC).

5. Let the bird rest for 15 to 20 minutes before carving.

Whole Turkey

Prep time: 25 minutes | Cook time: 2 hours | Serves 10 to 14

1 whole turkey
2 tablespoons olive oil
1 batch Chicken Rub

1. Supply your smoker with wood pellets and follow the manufacturer's specific start-up procedure. Preheat the grill, with the lid closed, to 350ºF (177ºC).

2. To remove the turkey's backbone, place the turkey on a work surface, on its breast. Using kitchen shears, cut along one side of the turkey's backbone and then the other. Pull out the bone.

3. Once the backbone is removed, turn the turkey breast-side up and flatten it.

4. Coat the turkey with olive oil and season it on both sides with the rub. Using your hands, work the rub into the meat and skin.

5. Place the turkey directly on the grill grate, breast-side up, and cook until its internal temperature reaches 170ºF (77ºC).

6. Remove the turkey from the grill and let it rest for 10 minutes, before carving and serving.

Turkey Breast with Garlic

Prep time: 5 minutes | Cook time: 1 to 2 hours | Serves 2 to 4

1 (3-pound / 1.4-kg) turkey breast
Salt and freshly ground black pepper, to taste
1 teaspoon garlic powder

1. Supply your smoker with wood pellets and follow the manufacturer's specific start-up procedure. Preheat the grill, with the lid closed, to 180ºF (82ºC).

2. Season the turkey breast all over with salt, pepper, and garlic powder.

3. Place the breast directly on the grill grate and smoke for 1 hour.

4. Increase the grill's temperature to 350ºF (177ºC) and continue to cook until the turkey's internal temperature reaches 170ºF (77ºC). Remove the breast from the grill and serve immediately.

Turkey Wings

Prep time: 5 minutes | Cook time: 1 hour | Serves 2

4 turkey wings

1 batch Sweet and Spicy Rub

1. Supply your smoker with wood pellets and follow the manufacturer's specific start-up procedure. Preheat the grill, with the lid closed, to 180ºF (82ºC).

2. Using your hands, work the rub into the turkey wings, coating them completely.

3. Place the wings directly on the grill grate and cook for 30 minutes.

4. Increase the grill's temperature to 325ºF (163ºC) and continue to cook until the turkey's internal temperature reaches 170ºF (77ºC). Remove the wings from the grill and serve immediately.

Turkey Drumsticks with Sugar

Prep time: 20 minutes | Cook time: 2½ to 3 hours | Serves 3

3 large fresh or thawed frozen turkey drumsticks

3 tablespoons extra-virgin olive oil

Brine:

4 cups filtered water

¼ cup kosher salt

¼ cup brown sugar

1 teaspoon garlic powder

1 teaspoon Poultry Seasoning

½ teaspoon red pepper flakes

⅛ teaspoon pink curing salt

1. Combine the brine ingredients in a 1-gallon sealable bag. Add the turkey drumsticks to the brine and refrigerate for 12 hours.

2. After 12 hours, remove the drumsticks from the brine, rinse them with cool water, and pat them dry with a paper towel.

3. Allow the drumsticks to air-dry, uncovered, in the refrigerator for 2 hours.

4. Remove the drumsticks from refrigerator and rub 1 tablespoon extra-virgin olive oil under and on the skin of each drumstick.

5. Configure your wood pellet smoker-grill for indirect cooking and preheat to 250ºF (121ºC) using hickory or maple pellets.

6. Place the drumsticks on the grill grates and smoke them at 250ºF (121ºC) for 2 hours.

7. After 2 hours, increase the grill temperature to 325ºF (163ºC).

8. Cook the turkey drumsticks at 325ºF (163ºC) until the internal temperature at the thickest part of each drumstick measures 180ºF (82ºC) with an instant-read digital thermometer.

9. Rest the smoked turkey drumsticks under a loose foil tent for 15 minutes before serving.

Turkey with Paprika

Prep time: 20 minutes | Cook time: 4 to 4½ hours | Serves 8 to 10

1 (10-pound / 4.5-kg) fresh or thawed frozen young turkey

6 tablespoons roasted garlic-flavored extra-virgin olive oil

6 tablespoons Sweet Dry Rub with Paprika or Poultry Seasoning

1. Trim away any excess fat and skin from the breast and cavity of the turkey.

2. Carefully separate the skin from turkey breast and leg quarters, leaving the skin intact.

3. Rub the olive oil inside the breast cavity, under the skin, and on the skin.

4. Generously season the breast cavity, under the skin, and on the skin with the rub or seasoning.

5. Configure your tailgate wood pellet smoker-grill for indirect cooking and smoking. Preheat to 225ºF (107ºC) using apple or cherry pellets.

6. Place the turkey, breast-side up, on the grill.

7. Smoke the turkey for 4 to 4½ hours at 225ºF (107ºC) until the thickest part of the turkey breast reaches an internal temperature of 170ºF (77ºC) and the juices run clear.

8. Rest the turkey under a loose foil tent for 20 minutes before carving.

Paprika Turkey Breast

Prep time: 20 minutes | Cook time: 3½ to 4¼ hours | Serves 6 to 8

1 (8 to 10-pound / 3.6- to 4.5-kg) bone-in turkey breast

6 tablespoons extra-virgin olive oil

5 tablespoons Sweet Dry Rub with Paprika or Poultry Seasoning

1. Trim away any excess fat and skin from the turkey breast.

2. Carefully separate the skin from the breast, leaving the skin intact. Rub the olive oil inside the breast cavity, under the skin, and on the skin.

3. Generously season the breast cavity, under the skin, and on the skin with the rub or seasoning.

4. Place the turkey breast in a V-rack for easier handling or directly on the grill grates, breast-side up.

5. Allow the turkey breast to rest at room temperature on your kitchen countertop while preheating your wood pellet smoker-grill.

6. Configure your wood pellet smoker-grill for indirect cooking and preheat to 225ºF (107ºC) using hickory or pecan pellets.

7. Smoke the bone-in turkey breast on the V-rack or directly on the grill grates at 225ºF (107ºC) for 2 hours.

8. After 2 hours of hickory smoke, increase the pit temperature to 325ºF (163ºC). Roast until the thickest part of the turkey breast reaches an internal temperature of 170ºF (77ºC) and the juices run clear.

9. Rest the hickory-smoked turkey breast under a loose foil tent for 20 minutes before carving against the grain.

Turkey with Sweet Dry Rub

Prep time: 20 minutes | Cook time: 3½ to 4¼ hours | Serves 8 to 10

1 (14-pound / 6.3-kg) fresh or thawed frozen young turkey

¼ cup roasted garlic–flavored extra-virgin olive oil

6 tablespoons Poultry Seasoning or Sweet Dry Rub with Paprika

1. Use poultry shears or a large butcher's knife to carefully remove the turkey's backbone by cutting along both sides of it.

2. Flatten the spatchcocked turkey by pressing down on the breast bone.

3. Trim away any excess fat and skin from the breast.

4. Carefully separate the skin from the breast, leaving the skin intact. Rub the olive oil inside the breast cavity, under the skin, and on top of the skin.

5. Season the breast cavity, under the skin, and on the skin with the seasoning or dry rub.

6. Configure your wood pellet smoker-grill for indirect cooking and preheat to 225ºF (107ºC) using hickory pellets.

7. Place the spatchcocked turkey skin-side down on a Teflon-coated fiberglass nonstick grill mat.

8. Smoke the turkey for 2 hours at 225ºF (107ºC).

9. After 2 hours, increase the pit temperature to 350ºF (177ºC).

10. Roast the turkey until the thickest part of the breast reaches an internal temperature of 170ºF (77ºC) and the juices run clear.

11. Rest the hickory smoked roasted turkey under a loose foil tent for 20 minutes before carving.

Buttery Turkey Breast

Prep time: 10 minutes | Cook time: 3½ to 4½ hours | Serves 8

1 (3- to 4-pound / 1.4- to 1.8-kg) whole turkey breast (with bone)
¼ cup poultry dry rub (with salt)
1 cup unsalted butter
1 package potato bun sliders (optional)
1 cup BBQ sauce, for serving

1. Prepare your Traeger by turning it to the SMOKE setting. Wait about 5 minutes for it to produce smoke, then set the Traeger to run at 250ºF (121ºC).

2. Remove the skin from the turkey breast and discard it. Rub the turkey breast liberally with your favorite poultry rub on all sides. Place the turkey breast on a disposable aluminum half-size tray and cover the tray with foil. Smoke for about 2½ hours, until lightly browned.

3. Remove the breast from the smoker and prepare two large sheets of heavy-duty aluminum foil (about double the size of the breast). Place the butter on top of the turkey breast and wrap tightly with both sheets of foil, one at a time, making sure the breast is completely covered.

4. Return the breast to the smoker for another 1 to 2 hours, or until an instant-read thermometer inserted into the center of the breast reads 160ºF (71ºC). Allow the turkey to cool slightly, then pull the meat apart using your hands or two forks.

5. Place the turkey on the sliders and top with your favorite BBQ sauce.

Turkey Patties with Onion

Prep time: 20 minutes | Cook time: 40 minutes | Serves 6

2 pounds (907 g) turkey minced meat
½ cup fresh parsley finely chopped
⅔ cup onion finely chopped
1 red bell pepper finely chopped
1 large egg at room temperature
Salt and pepper, to taste
½ teaspoon dry oregano
½ teaspoon dry thyme

1. In a bowl, combine well all ingredients.

2. Make from the mixture patties.

3. Start pellet grill on, lid open, until the fire is established (4 to 5 minutes). Increase the temperature to 350ºF (177ºC) and allow to preheat, lid closed, for 10 to 15 minutes.

4. Place patties on the grill racks and cook with lid covered for 30 to 40 minutes.

5. Your turkey patties are ready when you reach a temperature of 130ºF (54ºC).

6. Serve hot.

Turkey with Carrot

Prep time: 30 minutes | Cook time: 3 hours | Serves 5

4 cups applewood chips
1 fresh or frozen turkey, about 12 pounds (5.4 kg)
3 tablespoons extra-virgin olive oil
1 tablespoon chopped fresh sage
2½ teaspoons kosher salt
2 teaspoons freshly ground black pepper
1½ teaspoons paprika
1 teaspoon chopped fresh thyme
1 teaspoon chopped fresh oregano
1 teaspoon garlic powder
1 cup water
½ cup chopped onion
½ cup chopped carrot
½ cup chopped celery

1. Soak the wood chips into the water for about 1 hour; then drain very well.
2. Remove the neck and the giblets from the turkey; then reserve and discard the liver. Pat the turkey dry; then trim any excess of fat and start at the neck's cavity.
3. Loosen the skin from the breast and the drumstick by inserting your fingers and gently push it between the meat and skin and lift the wingtips, then over back and tuck under the turkey.
4. Combine the oil and the next 7 ingredients in a medium bowl and rub the oil under the skin; then rub it over the breasts and the drumsticks.
5. Tie the legs with the kitchen string.
6. Pour 1 cup of water, the onion, the carrot, and the celery into the bottom of an aluminum foil roasting pan.
7. Place the roasting rack into a pan; then arrange the turkey with the breast side up over a roasting rack; then let stand at the room temperature for about 1 hour
8. Remove the grill rack; then preheat the charcoal smoker grill to medium-high heat.

9. After preheating the smoker to a temperature of about 225ºF (107ºC).
10. Place 2 cups of wood chips on the heating element on the right side.
11. Replace the grill rack; then place the roasting pan with the turkey over the grill rack over the left burner.
12. Cover and smoke for about 3 hours and turn the chicken halfway through the cooking time; then add the remaining 2 cups of wood chips halfway through the cooking time.
13. Place the turkey over a cutting board; then let stand for about 30 minutes.
14. Discard the turkey skin; then serve and enjoy your dish!

Turkey Drumsticks

Prep time: 10 minutes | Cook time: 1 hour 25 minutes | Serves 2 to 4

2 turkey drumsticks
2 tablespoons olive oil
1 batch Chicken Rub

1. Supply your smoker with wood pellets and follow the manufacturer's specific start-up procedure. Preheat the grill, with the lid closed, to 180ºF (82ºC).
2. Coat the turkey drumsticks with olive oil and season all sides with the rub. Using your hands, work the rub into the meat and skin.
3. Place the drumsticks directly on the grill grate and smoke for 1 hour.
4. Increase the grill's temperature to 325ºF (163ºC) and continue to cook until the turkey's internal temperature reaches 170ºF (77ºC). Remove the drumsticks from the grill and serve immediately.

Turkey with Chicken Rub

Prep time: 25 minutes | Cook time: 2 hours | Serves 10 to 14

1 whole turkey

2 tablespoons olive oil

1 batch Chicken Rub

1. Supply your smoker with wood pellets and follow the manufacturer's specific start-up procedure. Preheat the grill, with the lid closed, to 350ºF (177ºC).

2. To remove the turkey's backbone, place the turkey on a work surface, on its breast. Using kitchen shears, cut along one side of the turkey's backbone and then the other. Pull out the bone.

3. Once the backbone is removed, turn the turkey breast-side up and flatten it.

4. Coat the turkey with olive oil and season it on both sides with the rub. Using your hands, work the rub into the meat and skin.

5. Place the turkey directly on the grill grate, breast-side up, and cook until its internal temperature reaches 170ºF (77ºC).

6. Remove the turkey from the grill and let it rest for 10 minutes, before carving and serving.

Tangy Turkey Breast with Lime

Prep time: 20 minutes | Cook time: 2 to 3 hours | Serves 10 to 12

1 turkey breast half, preferably bone-in (5 to 6 pounds / 2.3 to 2.7 kg)

1 lime, quartered

1 lemon, quartered and seeded

1 orange, quartered and seeded

¼ grapefruit, with rind, seeded and cut into 1-inch pieces

¼ cup coarse salt (sea or kosher)

¼ cup packed light or dark brown sugar

2 tablespoons cracked black peppercorns

1 tablespoon fennel pollen or fennel seeds

6 tablespoons extra virgin olive oil, or as needed

¼ cup water, or as needed

1. Rinse the turkey breast and blot dry with paper towels. If using a bone-in breast, trim off any visible rib tips. Place the turkey in a jumbo heavy-duty resealable plastic bag.

2. Make the citrus seasoning: Place the lime, lemon, orange, grapefruit, salt, sugar, pepper, and fennel pollen in a food processor and grind to a coarse paste. Grind in 4 tablespoons of the olive oil and ¼ to ½ cup of water—enough to make a thick but pourable paste. Pour this mixture over the turkey in the bag, massaging the bag to coat the meat evenly. Seal the bag and place it in a large aluminum foil pan to contain any leaks. Marinate the turkey in this mixture in the refrigerator for 24 hours, turning the bag over several times so the meat marinates evenly.

3. Drain the turkey on a wire rack over a rimmed baking sheet. For a finished look, scrape off the marinade; for a more rustic look, leave it on. Let it dry in the refrigerator for 2 hours.

4. Set up your smoker following the manufacturer's instructions and preheat to 225ºF (107ºC) to 250ºF (121ºC). Add the wood as specified by the manufacturer.

5. Place the turkey breast in the smoker. After 1 hour, start basting the turkey with the remaining olive oil, and continue basting every 45 minutes. Smoke until the outside is bronzed with smoke and the internal temperature of the meat reaches 165ºF (74ºC) on an instant-read thermometer. This will take 2 to 3 hours.

6. Transfer the turkey to a cutting board. To serve it hot, let it rest for 5 minutes, then thinly slice across the grain. To serve it cold (which is how we like it at my house), let the turkey breast cool to room temperature, then thinly slice. Store any extra in the refrigerator, where it will keep for at least 3 days.

CHAPTER 8: FISH AND SEAFOOD

Grilled Scallops

Prep time: 10 minutes | Cook time: 10 minutes | Serves 4

1 pound (454 g) large scallops

2 tablespoons olive oil

1 batch Dill Seafood Rub

1. Supply your smoker with wood pellets and follow the manufacturer's specific start-up procedure. Preheat the grill, with the lid closed, to 375ºF (191ºC).

2. Coat the scallops all over with olive oil and season all sides with the rub.

3. Place the scallops directly on the grill grate and grill for 5 minutes per side. Remove the scallops from the grill and serve immediately.

Salmon with Butter

Prep time: 15 minutes | Cook time: 1 hour 15 minutes | Serves 4

1 (2-pound / 907-g) half salmon fillet

1 batch Dill Seafood Rub

2 tablespoons butter, cut into 3 or 4 slices

1. Supply your smoker with wood pellets and follow the manufacturer's specific start-up procedure. Preheat the grill, with the lid closed, to 180ºF (82ºC).

2. Season the salmon all over with the rub. Using your hands, work the rub into the flesh.

3. Place the salmon directly on the grill grate, skin-side down, and smoke for 1 hour.

4. Place the butter slices on the salmon, equally spaced. Increase the grill's temperature to 300ºF (149ºC) and continue to cook until the salmon's internal temperature reaches 145ºF (63ºC).

Remove the salmon from the grill and serve immediately.

Salmon with Mayo

Prep time: 20 minutes | Cook time: 25 minutes | Serves 4

1 (2-pound / 907-g) half salmon fillet

3 tablespoons mayonnaise

1 batch Dill Seafood Rub

1. Supply your smoker with wood pellets and follow the manufacturer's specific start-up procedure. Preheat the grill, with the lid closed, to 325ºF (163ºC).

2. Using your hands, rub the salmon fillet all over with the mayonnaise and sprinkle it with the rub.

3. Place the salmon directly on the grill grate, skin-side down, and grill until its internal temperature reaches 145ºF (63ºC). Remove the salmon from the grill and serve immediately.

Salmon Fillets

Prep time: 15 minutes | Cook time: 4 to 6 hours | Serves 4

1 (2-pound / 907-g) half salmon fillet

1 batch Dill Seafood Rub

1. Supply your smoker with wood pellets and follow the manufacturer's specific start-up procedure. Preheat the grill, with the lid closed, to 180ºF (82ºC).

2. Season the salmon all over with the rub. Using your hands, work the rub into the flesh.

3. Place the salmon directly on the grill grate, skin-side down, and smoke until its internal temperature reaches 145ºF (63ºC). Remove the salmon from the grill and serve immediately.

Halibut Fillets

Prep time: 5 minutes | Cook time: 20 minutes | Serves 4

1 pound (454 g) halibut fillet

1 batch Dill Seafood Rub

1. Supply your smoker with wood pellets and follow the manufacturer's specific start-up procedure. Preheat the grill, with the lid closed, to 325ºF (163ºC).

2. Sprinkle the halibut fillet on all sides with the rub. Using your hands, work the rub into the meat.

3. Place the halibut directly on the grill grate and grill until its internal temperature reaches 145ºF (63ºC). Remove the halibut from the grill and serve immediately.

Tuna Steaks

Prep time: 10 minutes | Cook time: 10 minutes | Serves 2

2 (1½- to 2-inch-thick) tuna steaks

2 tablespoons olive oil

Salt and freshly ground black pepper, to taste

1. Supply your smoker with wood pellets and follow the manufacturer's specific start-up procedure. Preheat the grill, with the lid closed, to 500ºF (260ºC).

2. Rub the tuna steaks all over with olive oil and season both sides with salt and pepper.

3. Place the tuna steaks directly on the grill grate and grill for 3 to 5 minutes per side, leaving a pink center. Remove the tuna steaks from the grill and serve immediately.

Shrimp with Dill

Prep time: 15 minutes | Cook time: 10 minutes | Serves 4

1 pound (454 g) peeled and deveined shrimp, with tails on

2 tablespoons olive oil

1 batch Dill Seafood Rub

1. Soak wooden skewers in water for 30 minutes.

2. Supply your smoker with wood pellets and follow the manufacturer's specific start-up procedure. Preheat the grill, with the lid closed, to 375ºF (191ºC).

3. Thread 4 or 5 shrimp per skewer.

4. Coat the shrimp all over with olive oil and season each side of the skewers with the rub.

5. Place the skewers directly on the grill grate and grill the shrimp for 5 minutes per side. Remove the skewers from the grill and serve immediately.

Shrimp with Butter

Prep time: 10 minutes | Cook time: 20 minutes | Serves 4

1 pound (454 g) peeled and deveined shrimp, with tails on

1 batch Cajun Rub

8 tablespoons (1 stick) butter

¼ cup Worcestershire sauce

1. Supply your smoker with wood pellets and follow the manufacturer's specific start-up procedure. Preheat the grill, with the lid closed, to 450ºF (232ºC) and place a cast-iron skillet on the grill grate. Wait about 10 minutes after your grill has reached temperature, allowing the skillet to get hot.

2. Meanwhile, season the shrimp all over with the rub.

3. When the skillet is hot, place the butter in it to melt. Once the butter melts, stir in the Worcestershire sauce.

4. Add the shrimp and gently stir to coat. Smoke-braise the shrimp for about 10 minutes per side, until opaque and cooked through. Remove the shrimp from the grill and serve immediately.

Catfish Fillets

Prep time: 15 minutes | Cook time: 15 minutes | Serves 6

2½ pounds (1.1 kg) catfish fillets

2 tablespoons olive oil

1 batch Cajun Rub

1. Supply your smoker with wood pellets and follow the manufacturer's specific start-up procedure. Preheat the grill, with the lid closed, to 300ºF (149ºC).

2. Coat the catfish fillets all over with olive oil and season with the rub. Using your hands, work the rub into the flesh.

3. Place the fillets directly on the grill grate and smoke until their internal temperature reaches 145ºF (63ºC). Remove the catfish from the grill and serve immediately

King Crab Legs

Prep time: 5 minutes | Cook time: 10 minutes | Serves 4

8 King crab legs

Dipping sauce of your choice

1. Supply your smoker with wood pellets and follow the manufacturer's specific start-up procedure. Preheat the grill, with the lid closed, to 325ºF (163ºC).

2. Place the crab legs directly on the grill grate and grill for 10 minutes, flipping once after 5 minutes. Serve the crab with the mop on the side for dipping.

Trout with Lemon

Prep time: 10 minutes | Cook time: 1 to 2 hours | Serves 6

6 to 8 skin-on rainbow trout, cleaned and scaled

1 gallon orange juice

½ cup packed light brown sugar

¼ cup salt

1 tablespoon freshly ground black pepper

Nonstick spray, oil, or butter, for greasing

1 tablespoon chopped fresh parsley

1 lemon, sliced

1. Fillet the fish and pat dry with paper towels.

2. Pour the orange juice into a large container with a lid and stir in the brown sugar, salt, and pepper.

3. Place the trout in the brine, cover, and refrigerate for 1 hour.

4. Cover the grill grate with heavy-duty aluminum foil. Poke holes in the foil and spray with cooking spray.

5. Supply your smoker with wood pellets and follow the manufacturer's specific start-up procedure. Preheat, with the lid closed, to 225ºF (107ºC).

6. Remove the trout from the brine and pat dry. Arrange the fish on the foil-covered grill grate, close the lid, and smoke for 1 hour 30 minutes to 2 hours, or until flaky.

7. Remove the fish from the heat. Serve garnished with the fresh parsley and lemon slices.

Halibut Steaks with Cucumber

Prep time: 25 minutes | Cook time: 2 hours | Serves 6

4 (6-ounce / 170-g) halibut steaks

¼ cup extra-virgin olive oil

2 teaspoons kosher salt

1 teaspoon freshly ground black pepper

½ cup mayonnaise

½ cup sweet pickle relish

¼ cup finely chopped sweet onion

¼ cup chopped roasted red pepper

¼ cup finely chopped tomato

¼ cup finely chopped cucumber

2 tablespoons Dijon mustard

1 teaspoon minced garlic

1. Rub the halibut steaks with the olive oil and season on both sides with the salt and pepper. Transfer to a plate, cover with plastic wrap, and refrigerate for 4 hours.

2. Supply your smoker with wood pellets and follow the manufacturer's specific start-up procedure. Preheat, with the lid closed, to 200ºF (93ºC).

3. Remove the halibut from the refrigerator and rub with the mayonnaise.

4. Put the fish directly on the grill grate, close the lid, and smoke for 2 hours, or until opaque and an instant-read thermometer inserted in the fish reads 140ºF (60ºC).

5. While the fish is smoking, combine the pickle relish, onion, roasted red pepper, tomato, cucumber, Dijon mustard, and garlic in a medium bowl. Refrigerate the mustard relish until ready to serve.

6. Serve the halibut steaks hot with the mustard relish.

Salmon Lox with Cheese Bagel

Prep time: 20 minutes | Cook time: 6 hours | Serves 6

¼ cup salt

¼ cup sugar

1 tablespoon freshly ground black pepper

1 bunch dill, chopped

1 pound (454 g) sashimi-grade salmon, skin removed

1 avocado, sliced

8 bagels

4 ounces (113 g) cream cheese

1 bunch alfalfa sprouts

1 (3½-ounce / 99-g) jar capers

1. In a small bowl, combine the salt, sugar, pepper, and fresh dill to make the curing mixture. Set aside.

2. On a smooth surface, lay out a large piece of plastic wrap and spread half of the curing salt mixture in the middle, spreading it out to about the size of the salmon.

3. Place the salmon on top of the curing salt.

4. Top the fish with the remaining curing salt, covering it completely. Wrap the salmon, leaving the ends open to drain.

5. Place the wrapped fish in a rimmed baking pan or dish lined with paper towels to soak up liquid.

6. Place a weight on the salmon evenly, such as a pan with a couple of heavy jars of pickles on top.

7. Put the salmon pan with weights in the refrigerator. Place something (a dishtowel, for example) under the back of the pan in order to slightly tip it down so the liquid drains away from the fish.

8. Leave the salmon to cure in the refrigerator for 24 hours.

9. Place the wood pellets in the smoker, but do not follow the start-up procedure and do not preheat.

10. Remove the salmon from the refrigerator, unwrap it, rinse it off, and pat dry.

11. Put the salmon in the smoker while still cold from the refrigerator to slow down the cooking process. You'll need to use a cold-smoker

attachment or enlist the help of a smoker tube to hold the temperature at 80ºF (27ºC) and maintain that for 6 hours to absorb smoke and complete the cold-smoking process.

12. Remove the salmon from the smoker, place it in a sealed plastic bag, and refrigerate for 24 hours. The salmon will be translucent all the way through.

13. Thinly slice the lox and serve with sliced avocado, bagels, cream cheese, alfalfa sprouts, and capers.

Shrimp and Clam Paella

Prep time: 30 minutes | Cook time: 45 minutes | Serves 6

6 tablespoons extra-virgin olive oil, divided, plus more for drizzling

2 green or red bell peppers, cored, seeded, and diced

2 medium onions, diced

2 garlic cloves, slivered

1 (29-ounce / 822-g) can tomato purée

1½ pounds (680 g) chicken thighs

Kosher salt, to taste

1½ pounds (680 g) tail-on shrimp, peeled and deveined

1 cup dried thinly sliced chorizo sausage

1 tablespoon smoked paprika

1½ teaspoons saffron threads

2 quarts chicken broth

3½ cups white rice

2 (7½-ounce / 213-g) cans chipotle chiles in adobo sauce

1½ pounds (680 g) fresh clams, soaked in cold water for 15 to 20 minutes

2 tablespoons chopped fresh parsley

2 lemons, cut into wedges, for serving

1. Make the sofrito: On the stove top, in a saucepan over medium-low heat, combine ¼ cup of olive oil, the bell peppers, onions, and garlic, and cook for 5 minutes, or until the onions are translucent.

2. Stir in the tomato purée, reduce the heat to low, and simmer, stirring frequently, until most of the liquid has evaporated, about 30 minutes. Set aside.

3. Supply your smoker with wood pellets and follow the manufacturer's specific start-up procedure. Preheat, with the lid closed, to 450ºF (232ºC).

4. Heat a large paella pan on the smoker and add the remaining 2 tablespoons of olive oil.

5. Add the chicken thighs, season lightly with salt, and brown for 6 to 10 minutes, then push to the outer edge of the pan.

6. Add the shrimp, season with salt, close the lid, and smoke for 3 minutes.

7. Add the sofrito, chorizo, paprika, and saffron, and stir together.

8. In a separate bowl, combine the chicken broth, uncooked rice, and 1 tablespoon of salt, stirring until well combined.

9. Add the broth-rice mixture to the paella pan, spreading it evenly over the other ingredients.

10. Close the lid and smoke for 5 minutes, then add the chipotle chiles and clams on top of the rice.

11. Close the lid and continue to smoke the paella for about 30 minutes, or until all of the liquid is absorbed.

12. Remove the pan from the grill, cover tightly with aluminum foil, and let rest off the heat for 5 minutes.

13. Drizzle with olive oil, sprinkle with the fresh parsley, and serve with the lemon wedges.

Oysters with Cheese Butter

Prep time: 20 minutes | Cook time: 15 to 20 minutes | Makes 1 dozen

8 tablespoons (1 stick) unsalted butter, at room temperature

¼ cup shredded Parmesan cheese

2 garlic cloves, minced

3 tablespoons chopped fresh parsley

2 tablespoons Worcestershire sauce

2 tablespoons hot sauce

1 teaspoon cayenne pepper

1 dozen raw, shucked oysters in bottom shells; top shells discarded

1. Supply your smoker with wood pellets and follow the manufacturer's specific start-up procedure. Preheat, with the lid closed, to 225ºF (107ºC).

2. In a small bowl, combine the butter, Parmesan cheese, garlic, parsley, Worcestershire sauce, hot sauce, and cayenne pepper.

3. Top each oyster with 1 tablespoon of the compound butter.

4. Place the oysters in the smoker, close the lid, and smoke for 15 to 20 minutes.

5. Serve immediately with the remaining compound butter.

Bacon and Butter Scallops

Prep time: 25 minutes | Cook time: 25 minutes | Serves 4

2 pounds (907 g) sea scallops (about 20)

8 tablespoons (1 stick) unsalted butter

4 garlic cloves, minced

2 tablespoons freshly squeezed lemon juice

1 tablespoon lemon-pepper seasoning blend

10 slices bacon, cut in half

20 toothpicks, soaked in water for 20 minutes

3 teaspoons chopped fresh basil

Lemon wedges, for serving

1. Place the scallops on a jelly roll pan (a baking pan with low sides).

2. Supply your smoker with wood pellets and follow the manufacturer's specific start-up procedure. Preheat, with the lid closed, to 225ºF (107ºC).

3. On the stove top, in a small saucepan over medium-low heat, melt the butter and sauté the garlic in it.

4. Stir in the lemon juice and remove from the heat.

5. Baste the scallops with lemon butter and sprinkle with the lemon-pepper seasoning.

6. Wrap each scallop with a half slice of bacon and secure with toothpicks.

7. Using tongs, gently remove the scallops from the pan and place directly on the grill grate.

8. Close the lid and smoke for 25 minutes, or until opaque and firm with an internal temperature of 130ºF (54ºC).

9. Remove from the heat. Plate the scallops, remove the toothpicks, and sprinkle with the fresh basil.

10. Serve with lemon wedges.

Lobster Tails with Butter

Prep time: 30 minutes | Cook time: 45 minutes | Serves 4

4 (8-ounce / 227-g) lobster tails, fresh or frozen

1 cup (2 sticks) unsalted butter, melted

¼ cup freshly squeezed lemon juice

1 garlic clove, minced

2 tablespoons chopped fresh parsley, divided

2 teaspoons freshly ground black pepper

1 teaspoon salt

1 teaspoon red pepper flakes

1.   Prepare the lobster tails by cutting along the middle of the shell, front to back.

2.   Lift the meat from each shell gently, so it rests on the split shell, but be sure to keep it attached at the base of the tail.

3.   Make a slit down the center of the meat and place the lobster tails on a perforated pizza pan or Frogmat (or you can smoke directly on the grate).

4.   Supply your smoker with wood pellets and follow the manufacturer's specific start-up procedure. Preheat, with the lid closed, to 225ºF (107ºC).

5.   In a small bowl, combine the melted butter, lemon juice, garlic, 1 tablespoon of parsley, the pepper, salt, and red pepper flakes.

6.   Pour a tablespoon of the butter mixture over each lobster tail.

7.   Place the pan on the grill grate (or place the lobster tails directly on the grate), close the lid, and smoke for 1 hour, basting once with the butter mixture, until the meat is white and opaque, with an internal temperature of 130ºF (54ºC) to 140ºF (60ºC).

8.   Remove the lobster tails from the grill and plate. Sprinkle with the remaining 1 tablespoon of parsley and serve hot with the remaining butter mixture for dipping.

Creamy Cheese Shrimp and Grits

Prep time: 30 minutes | Cook time: 15 minutes | Serves 8

7 cups chicken stock

2 cups water

3 cups white grits

8 tablespoons (1 stick) unsalted butter, divided

4 ounces (113 g) cream cheese, softened

2 tablespoons minced garlic

2 teaspoons salt, plus more for seasoning

2 teaspoons freshly ground black pepper, plus more for seasoning

1½ pounds (680 g) tail-off large shrimp, peeled and deveined

¾ cup cream sherry (such as Harveys Bristol Cream Sherry)

1 cup heavy (whipping) cream

1 cup shredded Cheddar cheese

½ cup chopped scallions

1.   On the stove top, in a large pot over high heat, bring the chicken stock and water to a boil.

2.   Gradually add the grits to the pot, stirring constantly, to prevent lumps.

3.   Cook the grits on low for 25 minutes, then stir in 4 tablespoons of butter, the cream cheese, minced garlic, 2 teaspoons of salt, and 2 teaspoons of pepper.

4.   Supply your smoker with wood pellets and follow the manufacturer's specific start-up procedure. Preheat, with the lid closed, to 450ºF (232ºC).

5.   Melt the remaining 4 tablespoons of butter in a disposable pan on the grill grate.

6.   Season the shrimp with salt and pepper and add to the pan of butter, sautéing for 2 to 3 minutes on each side.

7.   Remove the shrimp from the pan but leave the pan on the grill and pour in the cream sherry, stirring until reduced by about half. Add the heavy cream, stirring until thickened.

8.   Fold the sherry-cream mixture into the grits.

9.   Serve the grits in individual bowls topped with the shrimp, Cheddar cheese, and scallions.

Shrimp Skewers with Lime

Prep time: 25 minutes | Cook time: 4 to 6 minutes | Serves 4

1 (13½-ounce / 383-g) can coconut milk

¼ cup rum

1 tablespoon maple syrup

1 tablespoon unsalted butter

¼ cup packed light brown sugar

1 teaspoon salt

1 teaspoon freshly ground black pepper

Juice of 1 lime

2 pounds (907 g) tail-on jumbo shrimp, peeled and deveined

16 metal or wooden skewers (if wooden, soaked in water for 30 minutes)

1.   In a medium bowl, make a marinade by combining the coconut milk, rum, maple syrup, butter, brown sugar, salt, pepper, and lime juice. Blend well. Reserve half of the marinade in another bowl and set aside.

2.   Toss the shrimp in the remaining marinade, cover, and refrigerate for 1 to 2 hours.

3.   On the stove top, in a small saucepan over low heat, warm the reserved marinade for about 10 minutes, stirring constantly, until the sauce is reduced and thick and syrupy. Remove from the heat.

4.   Supply your smoker with wood pellets and follow the manufacturer's specific start-up procedure. Preheat, with the lid closed, to 450ºF (232ºC).

5.   Thread 4 shrimp on each of 8 skewers, then double-skewer with the remaining skewers. Place the skewers directly on the grill grate, baste with the warm sauce, close the lid, and smoke for 2 to 3 minutes, or until pink.

6.   Flip the shrimp, baste again, close the lid, and smoke for an additional 2 to 3 minutes.

7.   The shrimp will be firm and opaque when fully cooked through—be careful not to overcook them. Remove from the heat and serve immediately.

Basil Mussels with Cheese

Prep time: 20 minutes | Cook time: 1 hour 30 minutes | Serves 2 to 3

1 cup water

1 cup white wine

2 pounds (907 g) mussels, cleaned and debearded

¾ cup extra-virgin olive oil, divided

½ cup grated Parmesan cheese

¼ cup fresh basil leaves

2 tablespoons pine nuts

1 tablespoon minced garlic

1.   On the stove top, in a large stockpot over medium-high heat, bring the water and wine to a boil, then add one layer of mussels. Steam for 1 to 2 minutes, or until the shells open, then remove the mussels and set aside. Discard any that do not open.

2.   Repeat this steaming process until all of the mussels have been steamed open. Strain the liquid and set aside.

3.   Remove the mussels from their shells with a knife and place the mussel "meat" back into the liquid to soak for 20 minutes off the heat. The mussels will cool slightly.

4.   Meanwhile, in a food processor, pulse ½ cup of olive oil, the Parmesan cheese, basil, pine nuts, and minced garlic until coarsely combined. Store the pesto in the refrigerator until ready to use.

5.   Supply your smoker with wood pellets and follow the manufacturer's specific start-up procedure. Preheat, with the lid closed, to 150ºF (66ºC) to 180ºF (82ºC), or the "Smoke" setting.

6. Place the mussels in a grill basket on the grate, close the lid, and smoke for about 1 hour 30 minutes.

7. Serve the mussels with the pesto.

Salmon with Olive

Prep time: 30 minutes | Cook time: 1 to 2 hours | Serves 10 to 12

2 cups packed light brown sugar

½ cup salt

¼ cup maple syrup

⅓ cup crab boil seasoning

1 (3- to 5-pound / 1.4- to 2.3-kg) whole salmon fillet, skin removed

¼ cup extra-virgin olive oil

1 (15-ounce / 425-g) can pitted green olives, drained

1 (15-ounce / 425-g) can pitted black olives, drained

3 tablespoons jarred sun-dried tomatoes, drained

3 tablespoons chopped fresh basil

1 tablespoon dried oregano

2 tablespoons freshly squeezed lemon juice

2 tablespoons jarred capers, drained

2 tablespoons chopped fresh parsley, plus more for sprinkling

1. In a medium bowl, combine the brown sugar, salt, maple syrup, and crab boil seasoning.

2. Rub the paste all over the salmon and place the fish in a shallow dish. Cover and marinate in the refrigerator for at least 8 hours or overnight.

3. Remove the salmon from dish, rinse, pat dry, and let stand for 1 hour to take off the chill.

4. Meanwhile, in a food processor, pulse the olive oil, green olives, black olives, sun-dried tomatoes, basil, oregano, lemon juice, capers, and parsley to a chunky consistency. Refrigerate the tapenade until ready to serve.

5. Supply your smoker with wood pellets and follow the manufacturer's specific start-up procedure. Preheat, with the lid closed, to 250ºF (121ºC).

6. Place the salmon on the grill grate (or on a cedar plank on the grill grate), close the lid, and smoke for 1 to 2 hours, or until the internal temperature reaches 140ºF (60ºC) to 145ºF (63ºC). When the fish flakes easily with a fork, it's done.

7. Remove the salmon from the heat and sprinkle with parsley. Serve with the olive tapenade.

Basil Shrimp Cheese Pizza

Prep time: 20 minutes | Cook time: 10 to 15 minutes | Makes 1 pizza

¾ cup extra virgin olive oil, divided

6 cloves garlic, chopped, divided

¼ cup cornmeal or all-purpose flour

1 pound (454 g) fresh pizza dough

1 pound (454 g) black tiger shrimp, peeled and deveined

½ cup freshly grated Parmesan

1½ cups shredded Mozzarella

1 cup fresh cherry tomatoes, chopped

1 cup fresh basil, chopped

1. Place a pizza stone in an unheated Traeger and set it to HIGH. Preheat for 30 minutes.

2. Mix ½ cup of the olive oil and 5 cloves of the chopped garlic until combined. Sprinkle cornmeal or flour onto a large cutting board or flat surface and work the dough into a 14- to 16-inch round shape.

3. Brush the olive oil mixture onto the pizza dough, covering as you would with a pizza sauce.

4. Slice the shrimp in half down the vein line and place them on the pizza, laying them flat in

a pattern to cover most of the dough. Top the dough and shrimp with the Parmesan cheese. Finally, add the shredded Mozzarella, being sure to cover the entire pie, as this is what will seal in the goodness.

5. Transport the pizza to the Traeger using the cutting board or a sheet pan turned upside down and place either on your preheated pizza stone or directly onto the grates. Close the smoker lid and allow to cook for 10 to 15 minutes, rotating halfway through the cooking process.

6. Meanwhile, mix the remaining ¼ cup of olive oil, 1 clove of garlic, chopped tomatoes and basil together in a small bowl. Drizzle the mixture over the pizza, slice and serve.

Salmon Fillet with Sauce

Prep time: 30 minutes | Cook time: 1 hour | Serves 6 to 8

1 (3- to 4-pound / 1.4- to 1.8-kg) salmon fillet, with or without skin

Lemon-Garlic Butter Sauce:

2 tablespoons unsalted butter

4 cloves garlic, minced

¼ cup lemon juice

3 tablespoons honey

1 teaspoon reduced-sodium soy sauce

2 teaspoons Dijon mustard

1 tablespoon chopped fresh parsley, plus more to serve

1 teaspoon salt

2 teaspoons onion powder

1 teaspoon paprika

½ teaspoon black pepper

Parmesan Topping:

½ cup Italian bread crumbs

3 tablespoons melted butter

½ cup grated Parmesan cheese

1. Preheat the Traeger to 275ºF (135ºC).

2. To make a pouch to cook the salmon in, roll out a piece of foil that extends inches past the length of your salmon (so you can fold up the sides). Lightly spray the foil with nonstick cooking spray. Place the salmon in the center of the foil (skin-side down if it has skin) and fold up all the sides of the foil snugly around the salmon.

3. To make the butter sauce, add the butter and the minced garlic to a medium bowl and microwave until the butter is melted. Whisk in the lemon juice, honey, soy sauce, mustard, parsley, salt, onion powder, paprika and pepper and pour evenly all over the salmon.

4. To make the Parmesan topping, whisk together the bread crumbs, butter and Parmesan until the butter is evenly absorbed. Pat the topping evenly over the salmon.

5. Place your salmon, in its pouch, on the grate of the Traeger for 60 minutes or until the internal temperature reaches 165ºF (74ºC).

6. Garnish with fresh parsley if desired and additional salt and pepper as needed. Serve immediately.

Honey Shrimp

Prep time: 15 minutes | Cook time: 8 minutes | Serves 6 to 8

¼ cup olive oil

½ teaspoon salt

¼ teaspoon black pepper

1½ pounds (680 g) shrimp, peeled and deveined

Marinade:

2 tablespoons minced garlic

1 teaspoon ground ginger

⅔ cup honey

3 tablespoons fresh lemon juice

1 tablespoon rice vinegar

1 tablespoon low-sodium soy sauce

4 teaspoons Asian chili paste

1. To make the marinade, in a medium bowl, whisk together the garlic, ginger, honey, lemon juice, rice vinegar, soy sauce and chili paste. Put a ½ cup of the mixture into a large freezer bag along with the olive oil, salt and pepper. Add the shrimp to the bag and massage to evenly coat. Place the bag in the refrigerator for 1 hour. Refrigerate the remaining marinade separately.

2. Set up your Traeger to run at 400ºF (204ºC). Drain the shrimp and discard the marinade. Thread the shrimp onto skewers.

3. Place the shrimp skewers directly on the grate of the grill and cook for 3 to 5 minutes on each side, or until shrimp has become pink and firm, being careful to not overcook.

4. Remove the shrimp from the grill and brush the shrimp with the reserved marinade. Serve any remaining marinade on the side as a dip.

Lemon Sardine Ciabatta

Prep time: 10 minutes | Cook time: 5 minutes | Serves 6

4 cloves garlic, chopped

½ cup extra virgin olive oil, divided

Juice from 2 lemons

1 teaspoon smoked paprika

6 fresh whole sardines (about 1 pound / 454 g), scaled and gutted

1 large ciabatta bread

2 tablespoons chopped fresh parsley

Coarse sea salt and fresh black pepper, to taste

1. Combine the garlic, ¼ cup of the olive oil, the lemon juice and paprika in a shallow baking dish. Add the sardines and flip to coat all sides with the marinade. Spoon some marinade into the cavity of the fish. Set the fish aside to marinate for 30 minutes.

2. Prepare your Traeger to run on HIGH.

3. Slice the ciabatta bread into 1-inch slices and grill until just crispy and grill marks appear.

4. Remove the fish from the marinade and grill the fish on the Traeger for 2 to 3 minutes per side, until charred.

5. Place each fish on a slice of the grilled bread. Drizzle generously with the remaining olive oil, sprinkle with the fresh parsley and season with salt and pepper to taste.

Oysters with Butter

Prep time: 30 minutes | Cook time: 15 to 20 minutes | Makes 24 oysters

24 fresh oysters in the shell

4 tablespoons (½ stick) unsalted butter, cut into 24 equal pieces (each about ½ teaspoon)

Smoked Bread, for serving

1. Set up your smoker following the manufacturer's instructions and preheat to 225ºF (107ºC) to 250ºF (121ºC). Add the wood as specified by the manufacturer.

2. While the smoker is heating, carefully shuck the oysters, discarding the top shells. Pass the knife under each oyster to release it from the bottom shell. Leave the oysters in the shells. Arrange the oysters on a shellfish grilling rack or a wire rack, taking care not to spill the juices. Place a piece of butter on each oyster.

3. Place the rack with the oysters in the smoker. Smoke until the butter is melted and the oysters are warm but not fully cooked, 15 to 20 minutes, or as needed. Serve with grilled bread.

Lemony Trout and Bacon

Prep time: 15 minutes | Cook time: 15 to 25 minutes | Serves 4

4 whole trout (12 to 16 ounces / 340 to 454 g each), cleaned

Coarse salt (sea or kosher) and freshly ground black pepper

8 to 12 sprigs fresh dill

3 lemons, 1 thinly sliced and seeded, 2 cut in half crosswise

2 tablespoons (¼ stick) cold unsalted butter, thinly sliced

8 strips thin-sliced artisanal bacon (like Nueske's, or make your own, here)

1. Set up your grill for direct grilling and preheat to high (450ºF / 232ºC). Lay the planks on the grill and grill until the underside is charred, 2 to 4 minutes. Let cool. If working on an offset barrel smoker, hold the planks with tongs over the fire in the firebox to singe them.

2. Rinse the trout inside and out under cold running water, then blot dry inside and out with paper towels. Make three diagonal slashes in each side of the trout with a single-edge razor blade or sharp paring knife. (This looks cool and helps the fish cook more evenly.) Generously season the trout inside and out with salt and pepper. Place a couple of dill sprigs, lemon slices, and butter slices in the cavity of each trout.

3. Tie 2 bacon strips to each trout, one on top, one on the bottom, using 4 pieces of butcher's string to secure them. Arrange the trout on the charred side of the grilling planks (align them on the diagonal) and place a lemon half on each plank.

4. Set up your smoker following the manufacturer's instructions and preheat to medium (350ºF (177ºC)—or as hot as it will go). Add the wood as specified by the manufacturer.

5. Smoke-roast the trout until the bacon is sizzling and crisp and the trout is cooked through (about 140ºF / 60ºC in the center), 15 to 25 minutes at 350ºF (177ºC), 40 to 60 minutes if your smoker runs cooler. Alternatively, direct grill the trout over a medium flame (this will take about 10 minutes). If the edges of the plank start to burn, spray with a squirt gun.

6. Serve the trout on the plank with the smoked lemon halves for squeezing.

Bluefish with Honey

Prep time: 20 minutes | Cook time: 30 to 60 minutes | Serves 3 to 4

1½ pounds (680 g) fresh skinless bluefish fillets

¼ cup honey

¼ cup coarse salt (sea or kosher)

1 tablespoon cracked black peppercorns

2 whole cloves

2 allspice berries

1 quart hot water

1 quart ice water

4 strips lemon zest (2 by ½ inch each; remove the zest with a vegetable peeler)

Vegetable oil, for oiling the rack

1. Run your fingers over the bluefish fillets, feeling for bones. Pull out any you find with kitchen tweezers. Trim off any dark red portions from the skin side of the fillets using a sharp knife. (This is where the "fishy" flavor resides.)

2. Place the honey, salt, peppercorns, cloves, allspice berries, and hot water in a large deep bowl and whisk until the honey and salt are dissolved. Whisk in the cold water and lemon zest. Add the fish, cover with plastic wrap, and brine in the refrigerator for 8 hours, turning

several times. (Alternatively, place the fish and brine in a resealable heavy-duty plastic bag. Place the bag in an aluminum foil drip pan or baking dish to contain any leaks.)

3. Drain the bluefish in a colander and discard the brine and lemon zest. Rinse the bluefish well under cold running water; drain well and blot dry with paper towels. Place on an oiled wire rack over a rimmed baking sheet. Let the bluefish air-dry in the refrigerator until the surface is tacky, 2 hours.

4. Set up your smoker following the manufacturer's instructions and preheat to 225ºF (107ºC) to 250ºF (121ºC). Add the wood as specified by the manufacturer.

5. Smoke the bluefish on its wire rack in the smoker until bronzed with smoke and cooked through, 30 to 60 minutes. To test for doneness, press it with your finger; the flesh should break into clean flakes. Alternatively, insert the probe of an instant-read thermometer through one end of the fish into the center. The internal temperature should be about 140ºF (60ºC).

6. Transfer the bluefish on its rack to a rimmed baking sheet to cool to room temperature, then wrap in plastic wrap and refrigerate until serving. It will keep for at least 3 days in the refrigerator.

Arctic Char with Lemon

Prep time: 10 minutes | Cook time: 30 to 60 minutes | Serves 3 to 4

1 cup maple sugar

½ cup coarse salt (sea or kosher)

1 tablespoon freshly ground black pepper

1 teaspoon finely grated lemon zest

1½ pounds (680 g) fresh arctic char fillets, skin on or off

Vegetable oil, for oiling the rack

1. Place the maple sugar, salt, pepper, and lemon zest in a bowl and mix well, breaking up any lumps in the sugar with your fingers. Spread ½ cup of the cure on a rimmed baking sheet. The salt should extend ½ inch beyond the edges of the fish on each side. Place the fillets on top, skin side down. Sprinkle the remaining 1 cup cure on top of the char, patting it into the flesh with your fingertips. Cover with plastic wrap and cure the fish in the refrigerator for 1 hour.

2. Run your fingers over the flesh side of the char fillets, feeling for bones. Pull out any you find with kitchen tweezers. Rinse the char fillets under cold running water. Drain the fillets and blot dry with paper towels. Arrange the fillets skin side down on an oiled wire rack over a rimmed baking sheet and let air-dry in the refrigerator for 30 minutes.

3. Set up your smoker following the manufacturer's instructions and preheat to 225ºF (107ºC) to 250ºF (121ºC). Add the wood as specified by the manufacturer.

4. Place the fish on its wire rack in the smoker. Smoke the fish until golden brown, crusty at the edges, and just cooked through, 30 to 60 minutes. To test for doneness, press it with your finger; the flesh should break into clean flakes. Alternatively, insert the probe of an instant-read thermometer through one of the ends of the fish into the center. The internal temperature should be about 140ºF (60ºC).

5. Transfer the fish to a wire rack over a rimmed baking sheet and let cool to room temperature, then refrigerate wrapped in plastic until serving. Serve it at room temperature or chilled. It will keep in the refrigerator for at least 3 days or in the freezer for several months.

Black Cod with Bay Leaves

Prep time: 15 minutes | Cook time: 30 to 60 minutes | Serves 4

1 tablespoon fennel seeds

1 tablespoon coriander seeds

1 tablespoon white peppercorns

3 bay leaves, crumbled

⅔ cup coarse salt (sea or kosher)

¼ cup granulated sugar

¼ cup packed light or dark brown sugar

2 pounds (907 g) black cod fillets (preferably skin on)

Vegetable oil, for oiling the rack

1. Heat a dry cast-iron skillet over medium heat. Add the fennel seeds, coriander, peppercorns, and bay leaves and roast, stirring, until fragrant and lightly browned, 2 minutes. Transfer to a small bowl and let cool. Grind the spices to a fine powder in a spice mill or clean coffee grinder. Return them to the bowl. Stir in the salt and both sugars.

2. Place the cure mixture on a large plate or platter. Crust each cod fillet on all sides with the cure, rubbing it into the flesh with your fingertips. Tightly wrap each fillet in plastic wrap and place on a rimmed baking sheet, skin side down. Refrigerate for 3 hours.

3. Rinse the cod fillets well under cold running water. Blot them dry with paper towels. Arrange the fillets on an oiled wire rack over the baking sheet and let air-dry in the refrigerator for 30 minutes.

4. Set up your smoker following the manufacturer's instructions and preheat to 225°F (107°C) to 250°F (121°C). Add the wood as specified by the manufacturer.

5. Place the cod on its wire rack skin side down in the smoker. Smoke the cod until golden brown, crusty at the edges, and just cooked through, 30 to 60 minutes. To test for doneness, press it with your finger; the flesh should break into clean flakes. Alternatively, insert the probe of an instant-read thermometer through one end of the fish into the center. The internal temperature should be about 140°F (60°C).

6. Transfer the cod on its rack to the rimmed baking sheet and let cool to room temperature. Run your fingers over the fillets, feeling for bones. Pull out any you find with kitchen tweezers. (The bones are easier to remove when the cod is cooked.) Refrigerate the smoked black cod until serving. It will keep in the refrigerator, wrapped in plastic wrap, for at least 3 days or in the freezer for several months.

CHAPTER 9: APPETIZERS AND SNACKS

Smoked Cashews

Prep time: 5 minutes | Cook time: 1 hour | Serves 4 to 6

1 pound (454 g) roasted, salted cashews

1. Supply your smoker with wood pellets and follow the manufacturer's specific start-up procedure. Preheat the grill, with the lid closed, to 120ºF (49ºC).

2. Pour the cashews onto a rimmed baking sheet and smoke for 1 hour, stirring once about halfway through the smoking time.

3. Remove the cashews from the grill, let cool, and store in an airtight container for as long as you can resist.

Easy Eggs

Prep time: 10 minutes | Cook time: 30 minutes | Serves 12

12 hardboiled eggs, peeled and rinsed

1. Supply your smoker with wood pellets and follow the manufacturer's specific start-up procedure. Preheat the grill, with the lid closed, to 120ºF (49ºC).

2. Place the eggs directly on the grill grate and smoke for 30 minutes. They will begin to take on a slight brown sheen.

3. Remove the eggs and refrigerate for at least 30 minutes before serving. Refrigerate any leftovers in an airtight container for 1 or 2 weeks.

Cheese with Crackers

Prep time: 5 minutes | Cook time: 2½ hours | Serves 4

1 (2-pounds / 907-g) block medium Cheddar cheese, or your favorite cheese, quartered lengthwise

1. Supply your smoker with wood pellets and follow the manufacturer's specific start-up procedure. Preheat the grill, with the lid closed, to 90ºF (32ºC).

2. Place the cheese directly on the grill grate and smoke for 2 hours, 30 minutes, checking frequently to be sure it's not melting. If the cheese begins to melt, try flipping it. If that doesn't help, remove it from the grill and refrigerate for about 1 hour and then return it to the cold smoker.

3. Remove the cheese, place it in a zip-top bag, and refrigerate overnight.

4. Slice the cheese and serve with crackers, or grate it and use for making a smoked mac and cheese.

Bacon and Crab Cheese Poppers

Prep time: 20 minutes | Cook time: 30 to 40 minutes | Serves 6 to 8

12 large jalapeño peppers

8 ounces (227 g) cream cheese, at room temperature

Finely grated zest of 1 lemon

1 teaspoon Old Bay seasoning, or to taste

8 ounces (227 g) crab meat, drained, picked over, and finely shredded or chopped

Sweet or smoked paprika, for sprinkling

12 strips artisanal bacon, cut crosswise in half

1. Set up your smoker following the manufacturer's instructions and preheat to 350ºF (177ºC). (Yes, I know this is hotter than the conventional low and slow method—it gives you

crisper bacon.) Add the wood as specified by the manufacturer.

2. Cut each jalapeño in half lengthwise, cutting through the stem and leaving it in place. Scrape out the seeds and veins; a grapefruit spoon or melon baller works well for this. Arrange the jalapeño halves on a wire rack, cut side up.

3. Place the cream cheese in a mixing bowl. Add the lemon zest and Old Bay seasoning and beat with a wooden spoon until light. Gently fold in the crab. Spoon a heaping tablespoon of crab mixture into each jalapeño half, mounding it toward the center. Sprinkle with paprika.

4. Wrap each jalapeño half with a strip of bacon (you want the filling exposed at each end). Secure the bacon with a toothpick and arrange the poppers in a single layer on the wire rack.

5. Place the wire rack in the smoker. Smoke the poppers until the bacon and filling are browned and the peppers are tender (squeeze them between your thumb and forefinger), 30 to 40 minutes.

6. Transfer the poppers to a platter. Let cool slightly before serving.

Honey Bread

Prep time: 10 minutes | Cook time: 1½ to 2 hours | Makes 1 loaf

2 cups unbleached all-purpose white flour or as needed

1 cup whole wheat flour or 1 additional cup white flour

1 teaspoon coarse salt (sea or kosher), plus extra for sprinkling

1¼ cups water, plus extra as needed

1 envelope (2½ teaspoons) dry yeast

2 tablespoons honey

1 tablespoon extra virgin olive oil, plus oil for the bowl, loaf pan, and top of the bread

1. Set up your smoker following the manufacturer's instructions and preheat it as low as it will go (200ºF (93ºC) or below). Spread out the flours and salt in a thin layer (not more than ¼ inch thick) in an aluminum foil pan or on a rimmed baking sheet. Place the water in another foil pan.

2. Place the pans in the smoker and smoke until the white flour is lightly browned on the surface and tastes smoky and the water tastes smoky. Total smoking time is 15 to 20 minutes for hot-smoking or 1 to 1½ hours for cold-smoking.

3. Let the flours cool to room temperature. The water should only cool to warm 105ºF (41ºC).

4. Place the smoked flours, smoked salt, and yeast in a food processor and process to mix. Add the honey, olive oil, and the smoked warm water. Process in short bursts to obtain a soft, pliable dough. If the dough is too stiff, add a little more warm tap water; if too soft, add a little more flour. Alternatively, you can mix and knead the dough by hand or in a stand mixer fitted with a dough hook. Turn the dough onto a lightly floured cutting board and knead by hand into a smooth ball.

5. Place the dough in a large lightly oiled bowl, turning it to oil both sides. Cover with plastic wrap and let the dough rise in a warm spot until doubled in bulk, 1 to 1½ hours.

6. Punch down the dough, knead it into an oblong shape, and place it in an oiled loaf pan. Cover with plastic wrap. Let the dough rise again until doubled in bulk, 30 minutes to 1 hour.

7. Meanwhile, set up a grill for indirect grilling and preheat to 400ºF (204ºC) or preheat your oven to 400ºF (204ºC). If your smoker goes up

to 400ºF (204ºC), you can bake the bread in it. No need to add wood—you've already smoked the flour.

8. Brush the top of the loaf with a little more olive oil and sprinkle with a little salt. Bake the loaf until the top is browned and firm and the bottom sounds hollow when tapped, 30 to 40 minutes. Transfer the loaf pan to a wire rack and let cool for 10 minutes. Remove the bread from the pan, cool for 10 minutes more, slice crosswise and serve warm. Serve with the smoked butter and smoked honey.

Tomato and Cucumber Gazpacho

Prep time: 30 minutes | Cook time: 1 hour | Serves 4

4 luscious red ripe tomatoes (about 2 pounds / 907 g), cut in half widthwise

1 medium-size cucumber, peeled, cut in half lengthwise, seeds scraped out

½ green or yellow bell pepper, stemmed, seeded, and cut into 2 pieces

½ red bell pepper, stemmed, seeded, and cut into 2 pieces

1 small sweet onion, peeled and cut lengthwise in quarters

1 clove garlic, peeled

3 tablespoons really good extra virgin olive oil, plus extra for drizzling

About 2 tablespoons red wine or Spanish sherry vinegar

½ cup water, plus extra as needed

Coarse salt (sea or kosher) and freshly ground black pepper, to taste

1 tablespoon chopped fresh chives or scallion greens

1. Arrange the tomatoes, cucumber, peppers, and onion, cut side up, in an aluminum foil pan. Add the garlic.

2. Set up your smoker for cold-smoking, following the manufacturer's instructions. Add the wood as specified by the manufacturer.

3. Place the vegetables in the smoker. Smoke until bronzed with smoke (dip your finger in one cut tomato—the juices should taste smoky), 1 hour, or as needed. The vegetables should remain raw.

4. Cut the vegetables into 1-inch pieces, reserving the juices. Place in a food processor and process to a coarse or smooth puree (your choice). Gradually add the reserved juices, oil, vinegar, and enough water (about ½ cup) to make a pourable soup. Work in salt and pepper to taste, plus a few more drops of vinegar if needed to balance the sweetness of the vegetables. Alternatively, place the vegetables and their juices, oil, vinegar, and water in a blender and blend to your preferred consistency. Season with salt, pepper, and more vinegar. The gazpacho can be made several hours ahead to this stage, covered, and refrigerated, but taste and re-season it before serving.

5. Ladle the gazpacho into serving bowls. Drizzle additional olive oil on top and sprinkle with the chopped chives.

Chicken Livers with White Wine

Prep time: 15 minutes | Cook time: 30 to 40 minutes | Serves 4

1 pound (454 g) chicken or turkey livers

1 cup hot water

1½ tablespoons coarse salt (sea or kosher)

1 teaspoon black peppercorns

½ teaspoon fresh or dried thyme leaves

1 cup ice water

½ cup dry white wine

Vegetable oil, for oiling the rack

About 1 tablespoon extra virgin olive oil

1 tablespoon butter or bacon fat, for pan-frying (optional)

1. Trim any green or bloody spots off the livers.

2. Make the brine: Place the hot water, salt, peppercorns, and thyme in a deep bowl and whisk until the salt dissolves. Whisk in the ice water and wine. When the mixture is cold, stir in the chicken livers. Brine, covered, in the refrigerator for 3 hours.

3. Drain the livers in a colander and blot dry with paper towels. Oil a wire rack and arrange the livers on it. Let dry in the refrigerator for 30 minutes. Lightly brush the livers with olive oil on both sides.

4. Meanwhile, set up your smoker following the manufacturer's instructions and preheat to 300ºF (149ºC). Add the wood as specified by the manufacturer.

5. Place the rack in the smoker and smoke the livers until cooked to taste, 30 to 40 minutes for pink in the center. (Make a slit in one of the livers to check for doneness.) Do not overcook.

6. You can serve the livers hot from the smoker. To add a little crunch to the exterior, melt the butter in a large skillet over high heat. Pan-fry the livers until seared and crusty, 1 to 2 minutes per side.

Chicken and Bean Cheese Nachos

Prep time: 20 minutes | Cook time: 12 to 15 minutes | Serves 6 to 8

8 cups tortilla chips

2 cups shredded smoked brisket or chicken

1 can (15 ounces / 425 g) black beans (preferably organic and low-sodium), drained well in a colander, rinsed, and drained again

12 ounces (340 g) finely grated mixed cheeses (like Cheddar, smoked Cheddar, Jack, and/or pepper Jack; about 3 cups)

4 fresh jalapeño peppers, stemmed and thinly sliced crosswise, or ⅓ cup drained pickled jalapeño slices

4 scallions, trimmed, white and green parts thinly sliced crosswise

2 to 4 tablespoons of your favorite hot sauce (I like Cholula) or barbecue sauce

¼ cup coarsely chopped fresh cilantro (optional)

1. Set up your smoker following the manufacturer's instructions and preheat to 275ºF (135ºC). Add the wood as specified by the manufacturer.

2. Loosely arrange one third of the tortilla chips in the grill skillet. Sprinkle one third of the shredded brisket, beans, cheese, jalapeños, and scallions on top. Shake on hot sauce. Add a second layer of these ingredients, followed by a third.

3. Place the skillet with the nachos in your smoker and smoke until the cheese is melted and bubbling, 12 to 15 minutes.

4. Sprinkle the cilantro on top, if using, and dig in. Yes—you eat the nachos right out of the skillet, so be careful not to burn your fingers on the rim.

5. Smoked Nachos on the Grill

6. Set up the grill for indirect grilling and preheat to medium-high 400ºF (204ºC). Place the nachos pan on the grate away from the heat and toss the wood chips on the coals. Indirect-grill until the cheese is melted and bubbling, 5 minutes.

Butter Chicken Wings with Peanuts

Prep time: 15 minutes | Cook time: ½ to 2 hours | Serves 4 to 6

3 pounds (1.4 kg) chicken wings (about 24 pieces)

½ cup finely chopped fresh cilantro

2 teaspoons coarse salt (sea or kosher)

2 teaspoons cracked black peppercorns

2 teaspoons ground coriander (optional)

2 tablespoons Asian (dark) sesame oil

Vegetable oil, for oiling the rack

6 tablespoons (¾ stick) butter

4 jalapeño peppers, thinly sliced crosswise (leave the seeds in)

6 tablespoons sriracha (or other favorite hot sauce)

¼ cup chopped dry-roasted peanuts

1. Place the chicken wings in a large bowl. Sprinkle in ¼ cup of the cilantro, the salt, pepper, and coriander, if using, and stir to mix. Stir in the sesame oil. Cover the bowl and marinate, refrigerated, for 15 to 60 minutes (the longer they marinate, the richer the flavor).

2. Meanwhile, set up your smoker following the manufacturer's instructions and preheat to 375ºF (191ºC). (If your smoker's incapable of reaching that temperature, preheat as hot as the smoker will go.) Add the wood as specified by the manufacturer.

3. Oil the smoker rack and arrange the drumettes on it. Smoke the wings until sizzling, brown with smoke, and cooked through, 30 to 50 minutes. At lower temperatures, for example, at 250ºF (121ºC), you'll need 1½ to 2 hours. In some smokers, the pieces closest to the fire will cook faster; if this is the case, rotate the pieces so all cook evenly. To check for doneness, make a tiny cut in the thickest part of a few of the wings. The meat at the bone should be white, with no traces of red. Do not overcook. Arrange the wings on a heatproof platter.

4. Just before serving, melt the butter in a cast-iron skillet on the stove over high heat. Add the jalapeños and cook until they sizzle and start to brown, 3 minutes. Stir in the sriracha and bring to a boil. Pour over the chicken.

5. Sprinkle the chicken with the peanuts and the remaining ¼ cup cilantro and serve at once with plenty of napkins.

Tomato and Corn Salsa with Lime

Prep time: 15 minutes | Cook time: 15 to 20 minutes | Serves 6 to 8

4 luscious ripe red tomatoes (about 2 pounds / 907 g), cut in half widthwise

4 jalapeño peppers, stemmed and cut in half lengthwise (seeded for a milder salsa; seeds left in for hotter)

2 ears sweet corn, shucked

1 small sweet onion, peeled and quartered

½ cup chopped fresh cilantro

¼ cup fresh lime juice (2 to 3 limes), or to taste

Coarse salt (sea or kosher), to taste

Tortilla chips, for serving

1. Set up your smoker following the manufacturer's instructions and preheat to 225ºF (107ºC). Add the wood as specified by the manufacturer.

2. Place the tomatoes and jalapeños (both cut side up), corn, and onion in the smoker. Smoke the vegetables long enough to impart a smoke flavor (but not so long that you cook them), 15 to 20 minutes. Transfer the vegetables to a platter and let cool to room temperature.

3. Lay the corn flat on a cutting board and slice the kernels off the cob using broad strokes of a

chef's knife. Transfer the corn kernels to a large bowl.

4. Coarsely chop the tomatoes, jalapeños, and onion by hand or in a food processor. Add to the corn and stir in the cilantro, lime juice, and salt to taste. The salsa should be highly seasoned. Transfer the salsa to a serving bowl. Serve with chips alongside.

Camembert with Pepper Jelly

Prep time: 10 minutes | Cook time: 10 minutes | Serves 4

1 Camembert or small Brie cheese (8 ounces / 227 g)

3 tablespoons pepper jelly, tomato jam, or apricot jam

1 large jalapeño pepper, stemmed and thinly sliced crosswise

Grilled or toasted baguette slices or favorite crackers, for serving

1. Set up your grill for smoke-roasting and preheat to medium-high 400ºF (204ºC).

2. If you're charring the plank (this step is optional, but it gives you a lot more flavor), place it directly over the fire and grill until singed on both sides, 1 to 2 minutes per side. Set aside and let cool.

3. Place the cheese in the center of the plank. Spread the top with pepper jelly using the back of a spoon. Shingle the jalapeño slices on top so they overlap in a decorative pattern.

4. Place the plank on the grill away from the heat and toss the wood chips or chunks on the coals. Smoke-roast the cheese until the sides are soft and beginning to bulge, 6 to 10 minutes.

5. Serve the cheese on the plank, hot off the grill, with a basket of grilled baguette slices or your favorite crackers.

Homemade Cheese

Prep time: 5 minutes | Cook time: 2 to 4 minutes | Serves 2 to 3

Vegetable oil, for oiling the grate

1 ball (8 to 12 ounces / 227 to 340 g) fresh Mozzarella, patted dry

Extra virgin olive oil (optional)

Coarse salt (sea or kosher) or fleur de sel, to taste (optional)

1. Place a small mound of charcoal in the smoker firebox or to one side of a kettle grill and light it. Brush and oil the grate. When the coals glow red, place the cheese in the smoke chamber (or on the side of the kettle grill opposite the embers), as far away as possible from the fire. Toss the hay on the coals and close the smoker or cover the grill. Smoke the cheese until it's colored with smoke (but not long enough to melt it), 2 to 4 minutes.

2. Slide a spatula under the cheese and transfer it to a plate to cool. Do not grab it when hot, or the deposit of smoke will come off on your fingers. Serve once it has cooled to room temperature, or refrigerate until serving. (For maximum flavor, let the cheese warm to room temperature before serving.) Drizzle with olive oil and/or salt, if desired, and serve.

Syrupy Bacon Pig Pops

Prep time: 15 minutes | Cook time: 25 to 30 minutes | Serves 24

Nonstick cooking spray, oil, or butter, for greasing

2 pounds (907 g) thick-cut bacon (24 slices)

24 metal skewers

1 cup packed light brown sugar

2 to 3 teaspoons cayenne pepper

½ cup maple syrup, divided

1. Supply your smoker with wood pellets and follow the manufacturer's specific start-up procedure. Preheat, with the lid closed, to 350ºF (177ºC).

2. Coat a disposable aluminum foil baking sheet with cooking spray, oil, or butter.

3. Thread each bacon slice onto a metal skewer and place on the prepared baking sheet.

4. In a medium bowl, stir together the brown sugar and cayenne.

5. Baste the top sides of the bacon with ¼ cup of maple syrup.

6. Sprinkle half of the brown sugar mixture over the bacon.

7. Place the baking sheet on the grill, close the lid, and smoke for 15 to 30 minutes.

8. Using tongs, flip the bacon skewers. Baste with the remaining ¼ cup of maple syrup and top with the remaining brown sugar mixture.

9. Continue smoking with the lid closed for 10 to 15 minutes, or until crispy. You can eyeball the bacon and smoke to your desired doneness, but the actual ideal internal temperature for bacon is 155ºF (68ºC) (if you want to try to get a thermometer into it—ha!).

10. Using tongs, carefully remove the bacon skewers from the grill. Let cool completely before handling.

Cheesy Sausage Balls

Prep time: 15 minutes | Cook time: 30 minutes | Serves 4 to 5

1 pound (454 g) ground hot sausage, uncooked
8 ounces (227 g) cream cheese, softened
1 package mini filo dough shells

1. Supply your smoker with wood pellets and follow the manufacturer's specific start-up procedure. Preheat, with the lid closed, to 350ºF (177ºC).

2. In a large bowl, using your hands, thoroughly mix together the sausage and cream cheese until well blended.

3. Place the filo dough shells on a rimmed perforated pizza pan or into a mini muffin tin.

4. Roll the sausage and cheese mixture into 1-inch balls and place into the filo shells.

5. Place the pizza pan or mini muffin tin on the grill, close the lid, and smoke the sausage balls for 30 minutes, or until cooked through and the sausage is no longer pink.

6. Plate and serve warm.

Corn and Crab Cakes

Prep time: 25 minutes | Cook time: 10 minutes | Makes 30 mini crab cakes

Nonstick cooking spray, oil, or butter, for greasing
1 cup panko bread crumbs, divided
1 cup canned corn, drained
½ cup chopped scallions, divided
½ red bell pepper, finely chopped
16 ounces (454 g) jumbo lump crab meat
¾ cup mayonnaise, divided
1 egg, beaten
1 teaspoon salt
1 teaspoon freshly ground black pepper
2 teaspoons cayenne pepper, divided
Juice of 1 lemon

1. Supply your smoker with wood pellets and follow the manufacturer's specific start-up procedure. Preheat, with the lid closed, to 425ºF (218ºC).

2. Spray three 12-cup mini muffin pans with cooking spray and divide ½ cup of the panko between 30 of the muffin cups, pressing into the

bottoms and up the sides. (Work in batches, if necessary, depending on the number of pans you have.)

3. In a medium bowl, combine the corn, ¼ cup of scallions, the bell pepper, crab meat, half of the mayonnaise, the egg, salt, pepper, and 1 teaspoon of cayenne pepper.

4. Gently fold in the remaining ½ cup of bread crumbs and divide the mixture between the prepared mini muffin cups.

5. Place the pans on the grill grate, close the lid, and smoke for 10 minutes, or until golden brown.

6. In a small bowl, combine the lemon juice and the remaining mayonnaise, scallions, and cayenne pepper to make a sauce.

7. Brush the tops of the mini crab cakes with the sauce and serve hot.

CHAPTER 10: DESSERTS

Cinnamon Apples with Currants

Prep time: 30 minutes | Cook time: 1 to 1½ hours | Serves 6

6 firm, sweet apples like Honeycrisps or Fuji
6 tablespoons (¾ stick) unsalted butter, at room temperature
¼ cup firmly packed dark brown sugar
¼ cup dried currants
¼ cup gingersnap crumbs, graham cracker crumbs, or ground almonds
½ teaspoon ground cinnamon
¼ teaspoon freshly grated nutmeg
1 teaspoon pure vanilla extract
6 cinnamon sticks (each 2 to 3 inches long)
3 large marshmallows, halved horizontally (optional)
Regular vanilla ice cream, for serving (optional)

1. Set up your smoker following the manufacturer's directions and preheat to 275ºF (135ºC).

2. Core the apples, but don't cut all the way through the bottom; the idea is to create a cavity for stuffing.

3. Beat the butter and brown sugar in a medium-size bowl until fluffy. Beat in the currants, cookie crumbs, ground cinnamon, nutmeg, and vanilla. Divide the filling evenly among the apples. Stick a cinnamon stick upright through the filling of each apple and place a marshmallow half on top, if using.

4. Arrange the apples on grill rings on the smoker rack or balance them directly on the smoker rack. Smoke the apples until the sides are soft, but not collapsing, 1 to 1½ hours. If the marshmallows start to brown too much, loosely tent the apples with aluminum foil. Serve the smoked apples hot with ice cream on the side, if desired.

Gingersnaps Butter Cheesecake

Prep time: 45 minutes | Cook time: 1½ to 2 hours | Serves 8 to 10

The Crust:
Vegetable oil, for oiling the pan
12 ounces (340 g) gingersnaps (about 36) or chocolate icebox cookies (about 36)
3 tablespoons light brown sugar
8 tablespoons (1 stick) unsalted butter, melted

The Filling:
4 packages (8 ounces / 227 g each) cream cheese, at room temperature
1 cup firmly packed light brown sugar
2 teaspoons pure vanilla extract
2 teaspoons finely grated lemon zest
1 tablespoon fresh lemon juice
2 tablespoons (¼ stick) unsalted butter, melted
5 large eggs
Burnt sugar sauce (optional)

1. Set up your grill for indirect grilling and preheat to medium-high 400ºF (204ºC). Or preheat your oven to 400ºF (204ºC). Lightly oil the springform pan with vegetable oil and wrap a sheet of aluminum foil around the outside.

2. Break the cookies into pieces and grind with the brown sugar to a fine powder in a food processor. You'll want about 1¾ cups of crumbs. Add the melted butter and run the processor in short bursts to obtain a crumbly dough. Press the mixture evenly across the bottom and halfway up the sides of the springform pan. Indirect-grill or bake the crust until lightly browned, 5 to 8

minutes. Transfer the pan to a wire rack and let cool.

3. Wipe out the food processor bowl. Add the cream cheese, brown sugar, vanilla, lemon zest, lemon juice, and butter, and process until smooth. Work in the eggs one by one, processing until smooth after each addition. (You can also use a stand mixer, beating the cream cheese mixture until smooth and beating in the eggs one at a time.) Pour the filling into the crust. Gently tap the pan on the countertop a few times to knock out any air bubbles.

4. Set up your smoker following the manufacturer's instructions and preheat to 225ºF (107ºC) to 250ºF (121ºC). Add the wood as specified by the manufacturer.

5. Place the cheesecake in the smoker. Smoke until the top is bronzed with smoke and the filling is set, 1½ to 2 hours. To test for doneness, gently poke the side of the pan—the filling will jiggle, not ripple. Alternatively, insert a slender metal skewer in the center of the cake; it should come out clean.

6. Transfer the cheesecake in its pan to a wire rack to cool to room temperature. Refrigerate until serving; the cheesecake can be made up to 8 hours ahead. Run a slender knife around the inside of the springform pan. Unclasp and remove the ring. (You'll serve the cheesecake off the bottom of the pan.) Let the cheesecake warm slightly at room temperature before serving.

7. If serving with the sauce, pour some of it over the cheesecake and the rest into a pitcher. Cut into wedges and pass the remaining sauce.

Apple Crisp with Bacon

Prep time: 30 minutes | Cook time: ¾ to 1 hour | Serves 8

The Filling:
2 strips artisanal bacon, like Nueske's or the Made-from-Scratch Bacon here, cut crosswise into ¼-inch slivers
3 pounds (1.4 kg) crisp, sweet apples like Honeycrisps or Galas
⅓ cup packed light or dark brown sugar, or to taste
1½ tablespoons all-purpose flour
1 teaspoon finely grated lemon zest
1 teaspoon ground cinnamon
Pinch of salt
3 tablespoons bourbon

The Topping:
8 tablespoons (1 stick) unsalted butter, cut into ½-inch pieces and placed in the freezer until icy cold
½ cup crushed gingersnap cookies or granola
½ cup all-purpose flour
½ cup granulated sugar
½ cup light or dark brown sugar
Pinch of salt
Regular vanilla ice cream, for serving (optional)

1. Set up your grill for indirect grilling and preheat to 400ºF (204ºC).

2. Fry the bacon in a 10-inch cast-iron skillet over medium heat, stirring with a slotted spoon, until crisp and golden brown, 4 minutes. Transfer the bacon to a large bowl. Pour off and reserve the bacon fat for another use. Don't wipe out or wash the skillet.

3. Peel and core the apples and cut them into 1-inch pieces. Add them to the bacon. Stir in the sugar, flour, lemon zest, cinnamon, and salt. Stir in the bourbon. Taste the mixture for sweetness, adding sugar as needed. Spoon the filling into the skillet.

4. Place the butter, cookie crumbs, flour, white and brown sugars, and salt in a food processor. Grind to a coarse mixture, running the processor in short bursts. Don't overprocess; the mixture should remain loose and crumbly like sand. Sprinkle the topping over the apples.

5. Place the crisp on the grill or smoker rack away from the heat. Add the wood to the coals and cover the grill. Smoke-roast the crisp until the topping is browned and bubbling, the apples are soft (they should be easy to pierce with a skewer), and the filling is thick, 45 minutes to 1 hour.

6. Serve the crisp hot off the grill or smoker. Extra points for topping it with Smoked Ice Cream.

Chocolate Cream Bread Pudding

Prep time: 30 minutes | Cook time: 30 to 45 minutes | Serves 8

1 loaf (1 pound / 454 g) brioche, cut into 1-inch cubes (about 8 cups)

3 cups heavy (whipping) cream

2 cups whole milk

1½ cups sugar

Pinch of salt

1 vanilla bean

8 ounces (227 g) bittersweet chocolate, coarsely chopped

4 large eggs

2 large egg yolks

1 teaspoon pure vanilla extract (1½ teaspoons if not using the vanilla bean)

Butter, for buttering the skillet

Smoked ice cream, for serving (optional)

1. Set up your smoker following the manufacturer's instructions and preheat to 225°F (107°C) to 250°F (121°C). Add the wood as specified by the manufacturer.

2. Arrange the brioche cubes in a single layer in an aluminum foil pan and place in the smoker. Smoke, stirring occasionally so the cubes smoke evenly, until firm and toasted, 30 to 45 minutes.

3. Meanwhile, make the custard: Place the cream, milk, sugar, and salt in a heavy saucepan. Cut the vanilla bean, if using, in half lengthwise, and scrape the tiny black seeds into the cream. Then, add the vanilla bean halves. Bring to a boil over medium heat, whisking until the sugar dissolves. Remove the pan from the heat. Remove the vanilla bean halves; you can rinse, dry, and reuse them. Whisk in half of the chocolate until melted. (Return the pan to low heat if the chocolate needs help melting.)

4. Place the eggs, egg yolks, and vanilla extract, if using, in a large heatproof bowl and whisk until smooth. Gradually whisk in the hot cream mixture. Add it little by little so as not to curdle the eggs. Add the smoked bread cubes and fold until the bread has absorbed most of the custard.

5. Butter the skillet and spoon in the pudding mixture. Sprinkle with the remaining chopped chocolate, pushing the pieces into the bread pudding with a fork.

6. Increase the heat of your smoker to 325°F (163°C). Some smokers won't go that high; if not, increase the heat to 275°F (135°C). Smoke the bread pudding until puffed and browned on top and the custard is set, 40 to 60 minutes at the higher temperature, 1 to 1½ hours at the lower temperature. (Insert a metal skewer into the center of the pudding—it should come out clean when the custard is set.)

7. Serve the bread pudding hot (à la mode with Smoked Ice Cream, if desired).

Egg Flan

Prep time: 20 minutes | Cook time: 1 to 1¼ hours | Serves 6

The Caramel:

1 cup sugar

¼ cup water

The Flan:

½ cup sugar

3 large eggs

2 large egg yolks

Pinch of salt

1¼ cups whole milk

1 cup half-and-half

1 regular or smoked vanilla bean, split, or 1 teaspoon pure vanilla extract

1. Place the sugar and water in a heavy saucepan. Cover the pan and cook over high heat for 2 minutes. Uncover the pan and reduce the heat to medium. Swirl the pan so the sugar browns evenly, but don't stir, and watch it carefully so it doesn't burn or become bitter. (If it does, you'll need to start over.) Cook until the syrup is dark golden brown and caramelized, 4 to 6 minutes. Remove the pan from the heat immediately. Take care not to get any molten sugar on your hands.

2. Carefully pour the caramel into the ramekins, rotating each to coat the bottom and sides with it. (Wear grill gloves if necessary to protect your hands and arms.) Breathe a sigh of relief; the hard part is over. Let the caramel cool until hard. Arrange the ramekins on a rimmed baking sheet.

3. Place the sugar, whole eggs, yolks, and salt in a large heatproof bowl, and whisk just to mix. Combine the milk, half-and-half, and vanilla bean, if using, in a heavy saucepan and heat over medium heat until very hot but not boiling. Slowly whisk the hot milk mixture into the egg mixture, ½ cup at a time. Strain into a large heatproof glass measuring cup, discarding the vanilla bean. (Or you can rinse it off, dry it, and reuse it another time). If using vanilla extract, whisk it in now. Let the custard cool slightly, then pour it into the caramel-coated ramekins.

4. Set up your smoker following the manufacturer's instructions and preheat to 225ºF (107ºC) to 250ºF (121ºC). Add the wood as specified by the manufacturer.

5. Place the baking sheet with the ramekins in the smoker and smoke until the custard is set, 1 to 1¼ hours. To test for doneness, poke one of the ramekins. When the flan jiggles (not ripples), it's cooked. The internal temperature measured on an instant-read thermometer should be 180ºF (82ºC).

6. Transfer the flans to a wire rack to cool to room temperature, then refrigerate for at least 4 hours or as long as overnight before serving.

7. To unmold, run the tip of a paring knife around the inside edge of each flan. Place a plate firmly over the ramekin, invert, and shake until the flan slips loose. Spoon any caramel left in the ramekin around the flan.

Banana Pudding

Prep time: 15 minutes | Cook time: 20 minutes | Serves 6 to 8

1½ cups sugar

1 (14-ounce / 397-g) can sweetened evaporated milk

2 cups whole milk

4 eggs, separated (reserve egg whites for meringue, if using)

3 tablespoons all-purpose flour, sifted

½ (12-ounce / 340-g) box vanilla wafers (reserve a few for crumbled topping)

4 ripe bananas, thinly sliced

1 teaspoon cream of tartar (for meringue, if using)

1. In a medium saucepan over medium heat, combine the sugar and both milks. Stir until the sugar is completely dissolved. Turn the heat to low.

2. Add the egg yolks and flour to the pan. Stir until the mixture begins to thicken. Remove the pan from the heat and let the mixture cool.

3. In a large, clear ovenproof bowl or other serving dish, layer half of the cooled custard, then half of the vanilla wafers, then half of the bananas. Repeat the layers. Top with crumbled vanilla wafers. The pudding may also be topped with a meringue, if desired. Set the dish aside.

4. Preheat the oven to broil.

5. Pour the reserved egg whites into a large mixing bowl. Using a handheld electric mixer, beat the egg whites with the cream of tartar until stiff peaks form. Top the pudding with this meringue. Place the bowl on a lower rack under the broiler and cook for 2 to 3 minutes, until the meringue browns. Remove the pudding from the oven and enjoy.

Apple Crunch with Butter

Prep time: 13 minutes | Cook time: 40 to 45 minutes | Serves 6

4 cups peeled, cored, and sliced apples, preferably Granny Smith

¾ cup all-purpose flour

1 cup sugar

1 teaspoon ground cinnamon

½ teaspoon salt

8 tablespoons (1 stick) unsalted butter, cut into pieces, at room temperature, plus extra for the baking dish

Vanilla ice cream (optional)

1. Preheat the oven to 350ºF (177ºC).

2. Lightly butter a 9-inch square baking dish. Place the apple slices in the baking dish.

3. In the bowl of a food processor, combine the flour, sugar, cinnamon, and salt. Pulse a couple of times to combine. Add the butter and pulse until the mixture resembles coarse crumbs.

4. Sprinkle the crumb mixture over the apples.

5. Bake for 40 to 45 minutes, until the apples are tender. Serve warm, with ice cream, if you like.

Peaches with Butter and Apricot

Prep time: 8 minutes | Cook time: 10 minutes | Serves 4

4 fresh ripe Georgia peaches

8 tablespoons (1 stick) unsalted butter

1 cup (packed) dark brown sugar

1 ounce (28 g) (2 tablespoons) dark rum

10 ounces (283 g) (1¼ cups) apricot preserves

Vanilla ice cream (optional)

1. Heat a smoker to 325ºF (163ºC).

2. Pit the peaches and cut each one into quarters. Place the quarters on skewers. Lay the skewers on a large aluminum pan.

3. In a small saucepan over medium-low heat, combine the butter, brown sugar, rum, and preserves. Stir to thoroughly combine.

4. Glaze the peaches with the preserves mixture, place the pan in the smoker, and cook for 4 minutes on each side or until the peaches are soft. Serve the peaches atop vanilla ice cream, if you like.

Bacon and Chocolate Cookies

Prep time: 20 minutes | Cook time: 10 to 12 minutes | Makes 2 dounceen cookies

2¾ cups all-purpose flour

1½ teaspoons baking soda

½ teaspoon salt

12 tablespoons (1½ sticks) unsalted butter, softened

1 cup light brown sugar

1 cup granulated sugar

2 eggs, at room temperature

2½ teaspoons apple cider vinegar

1 teaspoon vanilla extract

2 cups semisweet chocolate chips

8 slices bacon, cooked and crumbled

1. In a large bowl, combine the flour, baking soda, and salt, and mix well.

2. In a separate large bowl, using an electric mixer on medium speed, cream the butter and sugars. Reduce the speed to low and mix in the eggs, vinegar, and vanilla.

3. With the mixer speed still on low, slowly incorporate the dry ingredients, chocolate chips, and bacon pieces.

4. Supply your smoker with wood pellets and follow the manufacturer's specific start-up procedure. Preheat, with the lid closed, to 375ºF (191ºC).

5. Line a large baking sheet with parchment paper.

6. Drop rounded teaspoonfuls of cookie batter onto the prepared baking sheet and place on the grill grate. Close the lid and smoke for 10 to 12 minutes, or until the cookies are browned around the edges.

Marshmallow Chocolate Dip Skillet

Prep time: 5 minutes | Cook time: 6 to 8 minutes | Serves 4 to 6

2 tablespoons salted butter, melted

¼ cup milk

12 ounces (340 g) semisweet chocolate chips

16 ounces (454 g) Jet-Puffed marshmallows

Graham crackers and apple wedges, for serving

1. Supply your smoker with wood pellets and follow the manufacturer's specific start-up procedure. Preheat, with the lid closed, to 450ºF (232ºC).

2. Place a cast iron skillet on the preheated grill grate and pour in the melted butter and milk, stirring for about 1 minute.

3. Once the mixture starts to heat, top with the chocolate chips in an even layer and arrange the marshmallows standing up to cover all of the chocolate.

4. Close the lid and smoke for 5 to 7 minutes, or until the marshmallows are lightly toasted.

5. Remove from the heat and serve immediately with graham crackers and apple wedges for dipping.

Blackberry Butter Pie

Prep time: 15 minutes | Cook time: 20 to 25 minutes | Serves 4 to 6

Nonstick cooking spray or butter, for greasing

1 box (2 sheets) refrigerated piecrusts

8 tablespoons (1 stick) unsalted butter, melted, plus 8 tablespoons (1 stick) cut into pieces

½ cup all-purpose flour

2 cups sugar, divided

2 pints blackberries

½ cup milk

Vanilla ice cream, for serving

1. Supply your smoker with wood pellets and follow the manufacturer's specific start-up procedure. Preheat, with the lid closed, to 375ºF (191ºC).

2. Coat a cast iron skillet with cooking spray.

3. Unroll 1 refrigerated piecrust and place in the bottom and up the side of the skillet. Using a fork, poke holes in the crust in several places.

4. Set the skillet on the grill grate, close the lid, and smoke for 5 minutes, or until lightly browned. Remove from the grill and set aside.

5. In a large bowl, combine the stick of melted butter with the flour and 1½ cups of sugar.

6. Add the blackberries to the flour-sugar mixture and toss until well coated.

7. Spread the berry mixture evenly in the skillet and sprinkle the milk on top. Scatter half of the cut pieces of butter randomly over the mixture.

8. Unroll the remaining piecrust and place it over the top of skillet or slice the dough into even strips and weave it into a lattice. Scatter the remaining pieces of butter along the top of the crust.

9. Sprinkle the remaining ½ cup of sugar on top of the crust and return the skillet to the smoker.

10. Close the lid and smoke for 15 to 20 minutes, or until bubbly and brown on top. It may be necessary to use some aluminum foil around the edges near the end of the cooking time to prevent the crust from burning.

11. Serve the pie hot with vanilla ice cream.

Carrot Cheese Cake with Pecan

Prep time: 20 minutes | Cook time: 1 hour | Serves 4 to 6

8 carrots, peeled and grated

4 eggs, at room temperature

1 cup vegetable oil

½ cup milk

1 teaspoon vanilla extract

2 cups sugar

2 cups self-rising or cake flour

2 teaspoons baking soda

1 teaspoon salt

1 cup finely chopped pecans

Nonstick cooking spray or butter, for greasing

8 ounces (227 g) cream cheese

1 cup confectioners' sugar

8 tablespoons (1 stick) unsalted butter, at room temperature

1 teaspoon vanilla extract

½ teaspoon salt

2 tablespoons to ¼ cup milk

The Cake

1. Supply your smoker with wood pellets and follow the manufacturer's specific start-up procedure. Preheat, with the lid closed, to 350ºF (177ºC).

2. In a food processor or blender, combine the grated carrots, eggs, oil, milk, vanilla, and process until the carrots are finely minced.

3. In a large mixing bowl, combine the sugar, flour, baking soda, and salt.

4. Add the carrot mixture to the flour mixture and stir until well incorporated. Fold in the chopped pecans.

5. Coat a 9-by-13-inch baking pan with cooking spray.

6. Pour the batter into prepared pan and place on the grill grate. Close the lid and smoke for about 1 hour, or until a toothpick inserted in the center comes out clean.

7. Remove the cake from the grill and let cool completely.

The Frosting

8. Using an electric mixer on low speed, beat the cream cheese, confectioners' sugar, butter, vanilla, and salt, adding two tablespoons to ¼ cup of milk to thin the frosting as needed.

9. Frost the cooled cake and slice to serve.

Lemon and Butter Bars

Prep time: 30 minutes | Cook time: 1 hour | Serves 8 to 12

¾ cup lemon juice

1½ cup sugar

2 eggs

3 egg yolk

1½ teaspoon cornstarch

4 tablespoon unsalted butter

¼ cup olive oil

½ tablespoon lemon zest

1¼ cup flour

¼ cup granulated sugar

3 tablespoon confectioner's sugar

1 teaspoon lemon zest

¼ teaspoon fine sea salt

10 tablespoon unsalted butter, cut into cubes

1. When ready to cook, set grill temperature to 180°F and preheat, lid closed for 15 minutes.

2. In a small mixing bowl, whisk together lemon juice, sugar, eggs and yolks, cornstarch and fine sea salt. Pour into a sheet tray or cake pan and place on grill. Smoke for 30 minutes whisking mixture halfway through smoking. Remove from grill and set aside.

3. Pour mixture into a small saucepan. Place on stove top set to medium heat until boiling. Once boiling, boil for 60 seconds. Remove from heat and strain through a mesh strainer into a bowl. Whisk in cold butter, olive oil, and lemon zest.

4. To make a crust, pulse together the flour, granulated sugar, confectioners' sugar, lemon zest and salt in a food processor. Add butter and pulse until just mixed into a crumbly dough. Press dough into a prepared 9" by 9" baking dish lined with parchment paper that is long enough to hang over 2 of the sides.

5. When ready to cook, set the Traeger to 350°F and preheat, lid closed for 15 minutes.

6. Bake until crust is very lightly golden brown, about 30 to 35 minutes.

7. Remove from grill and pour the lemon filling over the crust. Return to grill and continue to bake until filling is just set about 15 to 20 minutes.

8. Allow to cool at room temperature, then refrigerate until chilled before slicing into bars. Sprinkle with confectioners' sugar and flaky sea salt right before serving. Enjoy!

Chocolate Butter Brownie Pie

Prep time: 20 minutes | Cook time: 45 minutes | Serves 8 to 12

½ cup Semisweet chocolate chips

1 cup butter

1 cup brown sugar

1 cup sugar

4 whole eggs

2 teaspoon vanilla extract

2 cups all-purpose flour

½ cup cocoa powder, unsweetened

1 teaspoon baking soda

1 teaspoon salt

1 cup Semisweet chocolate chips

¾ cup white chocolate chips

¾ cup nuts (optional)

1 (8 ounce / 227 g) whole Hot Fudge sauce,

2 tablespoon Guinness beer

1. Coat the inside of a 10-inch (25 cm) pie plate with non-stick cooking spray.

2. When ready to cook, set the grill temperature to 350ºF (177ºC) and preheat, lid closed for 15 minutes.

3. Melt ½ cup (100 g) of the semi sweet chocolate chips in the microwave. Cream together butter, brown sugar and granulated sugar. Beat in the eggs, adding one at a time and mixing after each egg, and the vanilla. Add in the melted chocolate chips.

4. On a large piece of wax paper, sift together the cocoa powder, flour, baking soda and salt. Lift up the corners of the paper and pour slowly into the butter mixture.

5. Beat until the dry ingredients are just incorporated. Stir in the remaining semi sweet chocolate chips, white chocolate chips, and the nuts. Press the dough into the prepared pie pan.

6. Place the brownie pie on the grill and bake for 45-50 minutes or until the pie is set in the middle. Rotate the pan halfway through cooking. If the top or edges begin to brown, cover the top with a piece of aluminum foil.

7. In a microwave-safe measuring cup, heat the fudge sauce in the microwave. Stir in the Guinness.

8. Once the brownie pie is done, allow to sit for 20 minutes. Slice into wedges and top with the fudge sauce. Enjoy.

Buttermilk Cheese Muffins

Prep time: 15 minutes | Cook time: 12 to 15 minutes | Makes 3 dounceens mini muffins

1 package butter cake mix
1 package Jiffy Corn Muffin Mix
1 cup self-rising or cake flour
12 tablespoons (1½ sticks) unsalted butter, softened, plus 8 tablespoons (1 stick) melted
3½ cups shredded Cheddar cheese
2 eggs, beaten, at room temperature
2¼ cups buttermilk
Nonstick cooking spray or butter, for greasing
¼ cup packed brown sugar

1. Supply your smoker with wood pellets and follow the manufacturer's specific start-up procedure. Preheat, with the lid closed, to 375ºF (191ºC).

2. In a large mixing bowl, combine the cake mix, corn muffin mix, and flour.

3. Slice the 1½ sticks of softened butter into pieces and cut into the dry ingredients. Add the cheese and mix thoroughly.

4. In a medium bowl, combine the eggs and buttermilk, then add to the dry ingredients, stirring until well blended.

5. Coat three 12-cup mini muffin pans with cooking spray and spoon ¼ cup of batter into each cup.

6. Transfer the pans to the grill, close the lid, and smoke, monitoring closely, for 12 to 15 minutes, or until the muffins are lightly browned.

7. While the muffins are cooking, make the topping: In a small bowl, stir together the remaining 1 stick of melted butter and the brown sugar until well combined.

8. Remove the muffins from the grill. Brush the tops with the sweet butter and serve warm.

Berry Cream Cake

Prep time: 20 minutes | Cook time: 20 minutes | Serves 6

Bourbon Whipped Cream:
1 cup (240 ml) heavy whipping cream
2 tablespoons (16 g) powdered sugar
2 tablespoons (30 ml) high-quality bourbon
Berry Topping:

4 cups (1 kg) fresh or frounceen berries of choice (I like strawberries, blueberries and raspberries), chopped
3 tablespoons (38 g) granulated sugar
1 tablespoon (15 ml) lemon juice
1 pound (454 g) cake, cut into 6 slices

1. Prepare your Traeger to run on HIGH.

2. To make the whipped cream, pour the heavy whipping cream into a medium bowl and with a handheld mixer, whip until soft peaks form (or use an electric mixer). Gradually add in the powdered sugar, whipping until soft peaks form. Gently fold in the bourbon. Place the bowl in the refrigerator until ready to serve.

3. To make the berry topping, in a small saucepan, combine the berries, granulated sugar and lemon juice. Place the pan on the smoker grates and let the mixture come to a boil. When the mixture is boiling, cook, stirring often and mashing with a wooden spoon to break down the berries, for about 10 minutes, until it has a syrup-like consistency. Remove the pot from the smoker.

4. Place the slices of pound cake onto the smoker grates and grill for about 2 minutes per side until grill marks are visible. Carefully flip the cake and grill the other side. Remove the cake from the smoker and place on a plate. Layer with a few spoonfuls of the berry topping, followed by a generous dollop of whipped cream. Serve immediately.

CHAPTER 11: JERKY

Beef Jerky

Prep time: 20 minutes | Cook time: 4 to 5 hours | Serves 6 to 8

1 (3-pound / 1.4-kg) corned beef brisket, rinsed and cut into ¼-inch-thick slices

1. Supply your smoker with wood pellets and follow the manufacturer's specific start-up procedure. Preheat the grill, with the lid closed, to 180ºF (82ºC).

2. Place the corned beef slices directly on the grill grate and smoke for 4 or 5 hours, until the jerky is dried but still bendable. Remove and serve or refrigerate in an airtight container for up to 2 weeks.

Chicken Jerky

Prep time: 15 minutes | Cook time: 5 to 6 hours | Serves 6 to 8

1 pound (454 g) chicken tenders, halved lengthwise

Salt and freshly ground black pepper, to taste

1. Supply your smoker with wood pellets and follow the manufacturer's specific start-up procedure. Preheat the grill, with the lid closed, to 180ºF (82ºC).

2. Season the chicken tenders all over with salt and pepper.

3. Place the chicken tenders directly on the grill grate and smoke for 5 or 6, hours until the jerky is dried but still bendable. Remove and serve, or refrigerate in an airtight container for up to 2 weeks.

Beef Roast Jerky

Prep time: 25 minutes | Cook time: 4 to 5 hours | Serves 6 to 8

1 pound (454 g) top round roast

Salt and freshly ground black pepper, to taste

1. Supply your smoker with wood pellets and follow the manufacturer's specific start-up procedure. Preheat the grill, with the lid closed, to 180ºF (82ºC).

2. Cut the roast against the grain into ¼-inch-thick slices.

3. Season both sides of the beef slices with salt and generously with pepper.

4. Place the beef slices directly on the grill grate and smoke for 4 or 5 hours, until the jerky is dried but still bendable. Remove and serve, or refrigerate in an airtight container for up to 2 weeks.

Garlic Beef Jerky with Sriracha

Prep time: 10 minutes | Cook time: 3½ to 4 hours | Makes 30 to 36 strips

2 pounds (907 g) lean beef (such as boneless sirloin, top or bottom round, or flank steak)

½ cup sriracha

¼ cup fish sauce or soy sauce

¼ cup Asian (dark) sesame oil

3 cloves garlic, peeled and minced

2 tablespoons chopped fresh cilantro

Vegetable oil, for oiling the rack (optional)

1. Wrap the beef in freezer paper or aluminum foil and freeze until firm but not frounceen solid, about 1 hour. (This facilitates slicing.)

2. Meanwhile, make the marinade: Place the sriracha, fish sauce, sesame oil, garlic, and cilantro in a large bowl and whisk to mix.

3. Using a sharp chef's knife, slice the beef along the grain into ⅛-inch-thick slices, trimming off any visible fat or connective tissue. Add the beef strips to the marinade, stirring to coat well on all sides. Cover with plastic wrap and marinate the beef strips in the refrigerator for at least 4 hours or as long as overnight—the longer they marinate, the spicier the jerky.

4. Cover a rimmed baking sheet with aluminum foil and place a wire rack on the foil. Remove the beef strips from the marinade and arrange them on the rack. Let drain and dry for 30 minutes.

5. Meanwhile, set up your smoker following the manufacturer's instructions and preheat to 160ºF (71ºC). Add the wood as specified by the manufacturer.

6. Remove the rack with the jerky from the baking sheet and place it in the smoker or arrange the beef strips on oiled smoker racks and smoke until dried but still flexible, 3½ to 4 hours.

7. Transfer the still-warm jerky to a large heavy-duty resealable plastic bag. (The resulting steam relaxes the meat.) Let cool to room temperature in the bag. Dig in now or later. Store the jerky in the refrigerator; it will keep at least a week.

Syrupy Bacon

Prep time: 20 minutes | Cook time: 40 to 60 minutes | Serves 15 to 20

½ cup (110 g) dark brown sugar

½ cup (120 ml) Grade A maple syrup

1 pound (454 g) bacon

1. Prepare your Traeger to run at 300ºF (149ºC). Line a baking sheet with parchment paper.

2. In a bowl, mix the brown sugar and syrup until combined. Lay the bacon in a single layer on the prepared baking sheet and brush generously with the sugar mixture. Flip the bacon and repeat on the other side.

3. Place the baking sheet with the bacon in the smoker and close the lid. After 20 minutes, flip the bacon and let it cook another 15 to 20 minutes until the sugar is melted and the bacon is cooked (note that the bacon will not be crispy when you remove it from the smoker).

4. Remove the pan from the smoker and let the bacon sit in the pan another 10 to 15 minutes to harden and finish the candying process. Remove the bacon from the pan and place in Mason jars or on a plate to serve.

Elk Jerky with Teriyaki Sauce

Prep time: 15 minutes | Cook time: 9 hours | Serves 14

5 pounds (2.3 kg) of elk hamburger

¼ cup of soy sauce

¼ cup of teriyaki sauce

¼ cup of Worcestershire sauce

1 tablespoon of paprika

1 tablespoon of chili powder

1 tablespoon of crushed red pepper

3 tablespoons of hot sauce

1 tablespoon of pepper

1 tablespoon of garlic powder

1 tablespoon of onion salt

1 tablespoon of salt

1. Mix all the ingredients for the seasoning with the elk hamburger into a large bowl and set it aside for about 12 hours

2. Light a charcoal smoker and let the temperature reach about 160° F; then make sure

that the temperature is about 225ºF (107ºC) during the smoking process

3. Remove the elk out of your refrigerator and start making jerking strips

4. Add smoker wood chips to your smoker; then rub a little bit of olive oil to the smoker

5. Rub 2 tablespoons of olive oil over the smoker grate and make sure the foil is very well coated with foil; then place the meat over the foil; the foil should be coated with oil too

6. Smoke the jerky for about 3 hours; then warm the dehydrator in the last 30 minutes of the smoking process

7. Line the prepared dehydrator with the smoked elk jerky meat and keep it in there for about 5 to 6 hours

8. Serve and enjoy your dish!

Beef and Pineapple with Sauce

Prep time: 15 minutes | Cook time: 12¼ hours | Serves 12

2 cups teriyaki sauce

1 cup of soy sauce

1 cup brown sugar

1 dash Worcestershire sauce

¼ pounds (113 g) fresh pineapple, peeled

2 garlic cloves

2 pounds (907 g) ground beef, cut into ½ inch strips

1. Take a large-sized bowl and add teriyaki sauce, brown sugar, soy sauce, and Worcestershire sauce

2. Add garlic and pineapple to a food processor and process until smooth

3. Pour the pineapple mixture into the sauce mix and stir, transfer the whole mixture to a re-sealable bag

4. Transfer the beef to the bag as well and coat it well, squeeze out as much air as possible and zip the bag

5. Store in your fridge and allow it to marinate for 6 to 8 hours

6. Add your desired wood Pellets to your smoker and heat it to 225ºF (107ºC)

7. Drain the beet from the marinade and transfer to your smoker

8. Smoke for 6 to 8 hours until the jerky is chewy but not crispy

9. Serve and enjoy!

Duck Jerky

Prep time: 30 minutes | Cook time: 5 to 6 hours | Serves 6 to 8

1 whole duck, skin removed

1 batch chicken rub

1. Supply your smoker with wood pellets and follow the manufacturer's specific start-up procedure. Preheat the grill, with the lid closed, to 180ºF (82ºC).

2. Remove the duck meat from the bones and cut the meat into pieces of your desired size.

3. Season the duck pieces with the rub and use your hands to work the rub into the meat.

4. Place the duck pieces directly on the grill grate and smoke at 180ºF (82ºC) for 5 or 6 hours, until the jerky is dried but still bendable. Remove and serve or refrigerate in an airtight container for up to 2 weeks.

Beef Jerky with Teriyaki

Prep time: 25 minutes | Cook time: 4 to 5 hours | Serves 6 to 8

1 pound (454 g) top round roast

1 batch Garlic and Soy Sauce Marinade

Salt and freshly ground black pepper, to taste

1. Cut the roast against the grain into ¼-inch-thick slices.

2. In a zip-top bag or shallow dish, combine the beef slices and marinade. Seal the bag or cover the dish and refrigerate the beef overnight.

3. Supply your smoker with wood pellets and follow the manufacturer's specific start-up procedure. Preheat the grill, with the lid closed, to 180ºF (82ºC).

4. Remove the beef slices from the marinade and season well with salt and pepper.

5. Place the beef slices directly on the grill grate and smoke for 4 or 5 hours, until the jerky is dried but still bendable. Remove and serve, or refrigerate in an airtight container for up to 2 weeks.

CHAPTER 12: RUBS, SAUCES AND MARINADES

Pork Rub

Prep time: 4 minutes | Cook time: 0 minutes | Makes ¼ cup

½ teaspoon ground thyme

½ teaspoon paprika

½ teaspoon coarse kosher salt

½ teaspoon garlic powder

½ teaspoon onion powder

½ teaspoon chili powder

¼ teaspoon dried oregano leaves

¼ teaspoon freshly ground black pepper

¼ teaspoon ground chipotle chile pepper

¼ teaspoon celery seed

1.   In a small airtight container or zip-top bag, combine the thyme, paprika, salt, garlic powder, onion powder, chili powder, oregano, black pepper, chipotle pepper, and celery seed. Close the container and shake to mix. Unused rub will keep in an airtight container for months.

Chicken Rub

Prep time: 5 minutes | Cook time: 0 minutes | Makes ¼ cup

2 tablespoons packed light brown sugar

1½ teaspoons coarse kosher salt

1¼ teaspoons garlic powder

½ teaspoon onion powder

½ teaspoon freshly ground black pepper

½ teaspoon ground chipotle chile pepper

½ teaspoon smoked paprika

¼ teaspoon dried oregano leaves

¼ teaspoon mustard powder

¼ teaspoon cayenne pepper

1.   In a small airtight container or zip-top bag, combine the brown sugar, salt, garlic powder, onion powder, black pepper, chipotle pepper, paprika, oregano, mustard, and cayenne. Close the container and shake to mix. Unused rub will keep in an airtight container for months.

Dill Seafood Rub

Prep time: 5 minutes | Cook time: 0 minutes | Makes 5 tablespoons

2 tablespoons coarse kosher salt

2 tablespoons dried dill weed

1 tablespoon garlic powder

1½ teaspoons lemon pepper

1.   In a small airtight container or zip-top bag, combine the salt, dill, garlic powder, and lemon pepper. Close the container and shake to mix. Unused rub will keep in an airtight container for months.

Cajun Rub

Prep time: 5 minutes | Cook time: 0 minutes | Makes 3 tablespoons

1 teaspoon freshly ground black pepper

1 teaspoon onion powder

1 teaspoon coarse kosher salt

1 teaspoon garlic powder

1 teaspoon sweet paprika

½ teaspoon cayenne pepper

½ teaspoon red pepper flakes

½ teaspoon dried oregano leaves

½ teaspoon dried thyme

½ teaspoon smoked paprika

1. In a small airtight container or zip-top bag, combine the black pepper, onion powder, salt, garlic powder, sweet paprika, cayenne, red pepper flakes, oregano, thyme, and smoked paprika. Close the container and shake to mix. Unused rub will keep in an airtight container for months.

Brown Sugar Rub

Prep time: 5 minutes | Cook time: 0 minutes | Makes ¼ cup

2 tablespoons light brown sugar

1 teaspoon coarse kosher salt

1 teaspoon garlic powder

1 teaspoon onion powder

1 teaspoon sweet paprika

½ teaspoon freshly ground black pepper

½ teaspoon cayenne pepper

½ teaspoon dried oregano leaves

¼ teaspoon smoked paprika

1. In a small airtight container or zip-top bag, combine the brown sugar, salt, garlic powder, onion powder, sweet paprika, black pepper, cayenne, oregano, and smoked paprika. Close the container and shake to mix. Unused rub will keep in an airtight container for months.

Sweet and Spicy Rub

Prep time: 5 minutes | Cook time: 0 minutes | Makes ¼ cup

2 tablespoons light brown sugar

1 teaspoon coarse kosher salt

1 teaspoon garlic powder

1 teaspoon onion powder

1 teaspoon sweet paprika

½ teaspoon freshly ground black pepper

½ teaspoon cayenne pepper

½ teaspoon dried oregano leaves

½ teaspoon ground ginger

½ teaspoon ground cumin

¼ teaspoon smoked paprika

¼ teaspoon ground cinnamon

¼ teaspoon ground coriander

¼ teaspoon chili powder

1. In a small airtight container or zip-top bag, combine the brown sugar, salt, garlic powder, onion powder, sweet paprika, black pepper, cayenne, oregano, ginger, cumin, smoked paprika, cinnamon, coriander, and chili powder. Close the container and shake to mix. Unused rub will keep in an airtight container for months.

Garlic and Soy Sauce Marinade

Prep time: 5 minutes | Cook time: 0 minutes | Makes 1 cup

¼ cup water

¼ cup soy sauce

¼ cup packed light brown sugar

¼ cup Worcestershire sauce

2 garlic cloves, sliced

1. In a small bowl, whisk the water, soy sauce, brown sugar, Worcestershire sauce, and garlic until combined. Refrigerate any unused marinade in an airtight container for 2 or 3 days.

Ketchup and BBQ Sauce

Prep time: 10 minutes | Cook time: 30 minutes | Makes 3 cups

1 small onion, finely chopped

2 garlic cloves, finely minced

2 cups ketchup

1 cup water

½ cup molasses

½ cup apple cider vinegar

5 tablespoons granulated sugar

5 tablespoons light brown sugar

1 tablespoon Worcestershire sauce

1 tablespoon freshly squeezed lemon juice

2 teaspoons liquid smoke

1½ teaspoons freshly ground black pepper

1 tablespoon yellow mustard

1.   On the stovetop, in a saucepan over medium heat, combine the onion, garlic, ketchup, water, molasses, apple cider vinegar, granulated sugar, brown sugar, Worcestershire sauce, lemon juice, liquid smoke, black pepper, and mustard. Bring to a boil, then reduce the heat to low and simmer for 30 minutes, straining out any bigger chunks, if desired.

2.   Let the sauce cool completely, then transfer to an airtight container and refrigerate for up to 2 weeks, or use a canning process to store for longer.

Chili Chicken Rub

Prep time: 5 minutes | Cook time: 0 minutes | Makes 2 cups

⅔ cup chili powder

½ cup sugar

4 tablespoons kosher salt

4 tablespoons onion powder

4 tablespoons garlic powder

1 teaspoon cayenne pepper

1.   In a large bowl, combine all the ingredients thoroughly. You can store this rub in an airtight container indefinitely.

Beef Rub

Prep time: 5 minutes | Cook time: 0 minutes | Makes ¾ cup

1 teaspoon kosher salt

2 tablespoons coarsely ground black pepper

1 teaspoon sugar

½ teaspoon chipotle pepper powder

½ teaspoon chili powder

1 teaspoon garlic powder

1 teaspoon granulated dried onion

1.   In a large bowl, combine all the ingredients thoroughly. You can store this rub in an airtight container indefinitely.

Tangy Ginger Rib Marinade

Prep time: 5 minutes | Cook time: 0 minutes | Makes 9 cups

1 liter ginger ale

1 quart orange juice

1¼ cups soy sauce

½ cups salt

2 (1-ounce / 28-g) packets dry ranch dressing mix

1.   In a large bowl, combine all the ingredients. Stir well to thoroughly incorporate. Pour into a large bottle or other container and store, refrigerated, for up to 2 weeks.

Hickory Sauce with Ketchup

Prep time: 10 minutes | Cook time: 0 minutes | Makes 3½ cups

2 tablespoons onion powder

2 tablespoons garlic powder

2 cups ketchup

2 tablespoons smoked sweet paprika

⅔ cup cider vinegar

2 tablespoons Worcestershire sauce

¼ cup (packed) dark brown sugar

2 tablespoons honey

2 tablespoons maple syrup

2 tablespoons kosher salt

2 tablespoons freshly ground black pepper

1.   Combine all the ingredients in a blender and pulse until thoroughly combined. Pour into a medium pot, and stir continuously over medium heat until heated through. Do not allow it to boil. Remove and use while hot.

2.   If reserving for a later use, allow the mixture to cool; then pour it into a large bottle or container and store, refrigerated, for up to 1 year.

Hot Vinegar Sauce

Prep time: 5 minutes | Cook time: 0 minutes | Makes 3½ cups

2 cups cider vinegar

1 cup ketchup

½ cup hot sauce

2 tablespoons salt

2 tablespoons coarsely ground black pepper

1 tablespoon red pepper flakes

½ cup sugar

1. In a stockpot over medium heat, combine the vinegar, ketchup, and hot sauce. Stir together. Pour in all the remaining ingredients and stir to dissolve. Do not boil. When the spices are thoroughly dissolved, take the pot off the heat, and funnel the sauce into a bottle. The sauce will keep, refrigerated, for up to 1 year.

Espresso Brisket Rub

Prep time: 5 minutes | Cook time: 0 minutes | Makes ½ cup

3 tablespoons coarse kosher salt

2 tablespoons ground espresso coffee

2 tablespoons freshly ground black pepper

1 tablespoon garlic powder

1 tablespoon light brown sugar

1½ teaspoons dried minced onion

1 teaspoon ground cumin

1. In a small airtight container or zip-top bag, combine the salt, espresso, black pepper, garlic powder, brown sugar, minced onion, and cumin.

2. Close the container and shake to mix. Unused rub will keep in an airtight container for months.

Molasses BBQ Sauce

Prep time: 5 minutes | Cook time: 30 minutes | Makes 3 cups

1 small onion, finely chopped

2 garlic cloves, finely minced

2 cups ketchup

1 cup water

½ cup molasses

½ cup apple cider vinegar

5 tablespoons granulated sugar

5 tablespoons light brown sugar

1 tablespoon Worcestershire sauce

1 tablespoon freshly squeezed lemon juice

2 teaspoons liquid smoke

1½ teaspoons freshly ground black pepper

1 tablespoon yellow mustard

1. On the stovetop, in a saucepan over medium heat, combine the onion, garlic, ketchup, water, molasses, apple cider vinegar, granulated sugar, brown sugar, Worcestershire sauce, lemon juice, liquid smoke, black pepper, and mustard. Bring to a boil, then reduce the heat to low and simmer for 30 minutes, straining out any bigger chunks, if desired.

2. Let the sauce cool completely, then transfer to an airtight container and refrigerate for up to 2 weeks, or use a canning process to store for longer.

Rosemary Lamb Seasoning

Prep time: 5 minutes | Cook time: 0 minutes | Makes 2 tablespoons

2 teaspoons dried rosemary leaves

2 teaspoons coarse kosher salt

1 teaspoon garlic powder

1 teaspoon freshly ground black pepper

½ teaspoon onion powder

½ teaspoon dried minced onion

1. In a small airtight container or zip-top bag, combine the rosemary, salt, garlic powder, black pepper, onion powder, and minced onion.

2. Close the container and shake to mix. Unused seasoning will keep in an airtight container for months.

Chimichurri Sauce

Prep time: 5 minutes | Cook time: 0 minutes | Makes 2 cups

½ cup extra-virgin olive oil

1 bunch fresh parsley, stems removed

1 bunch fresh cilantro, stems removed

1 small red onion, chopped

3 tablespoons dried oregano

1 tablespoon minced garlic

Juice of 1 lemon

2 tablespoons red wine vinegar

1 teaspoon salt

1 teaspoon freshly ground black pepper

1 teaspoon cayenne pepper

1. Using a food processor or blender, combine all of the ingredients and pulse several times until finely chopped.

2. The chimichurri sauce will keep in an airtight container in the refrigerator for up to 5 days.

Paprika Dry Rub

Prep time: 10 minutes | Cook time: 0 minutes | Makes ¾ cup

¼ cup paprika

¼ cup turbinado sugar

3 tablespoons Cajun seasoning

1 tablespoon packed brown sugar

1½ teaspoons chili powder

1½ teaspoons cayenne pepper

1½ teaspoons ground cumin

1. In a small bowl, combine the paprika, turbinado sugar, Cajun seasoning, brown sugar, chili powder, cayenne pepper, and cumin.

2. Store the rub in an airtight container at room temperature for up to a month.

Blueberry BBQ Sauce

Prep time: 5 minutes | Cook time: 10 minutes | Makes 1 cup

2 cups water

½ cup minced fresh blueberries

1 tablespoon balsamic vinegar

½ cup ketchup

1 tablespoon Worcestershire sauce

1 teaspoon Sriracha

1 teaspoon liquid smoke

1 teaspoon Dijon mustard

Salt and freshly ground black pepper

1. On the stove top, in a saucepan over low heat, simmer the water, blueberries, and balsamic vinegar for 5 minutes.

2. Stir in the ketchup, Worcestershire sauce, Sriracha, liquid smoke, and Dijon mustard, season with salt and pepper, and continue simmering for 5 minutes.

3. Remove from the heat and strain out most of the blueberry pulp.

4. The barbecue sauce will keep in an airtight container in the refrigerator for up to 1 week.

Sweet Dry Rub with Paprika

Prep time: 15 minutes | Cook time: 0 minutes | Makes 3 cups

1¼ cups sugar

¼ cup Lawry's seasoned salt

¼ cup garlic salt

¼ cup plus 1½ teaspoons celery salt

¼ cup onion salt

½ cup paprika

3 tablespoons chili powder

2 tablespoons black pepper

1 tablespoon lemon pepper

2 teaspoons celery seed

2 teaspoons dried ground sage

1 teaspoon dried mustard

½ teaspoon dried ground thyme

½ teaspoon cayenne pepper

1.   Place all the ingredients in a medium bowl and mix until well blended.

2.   Store in a cool area away from light in an airtight jar or sealable plastic bag.

Pork Dry Rub

Prep time: 15 minutes | Cook time: 0 minutes | Makes ¾ cup

¼ cup smoked paprika

¼ cup brown sugar

3 tablespoons kosher salt

2 tablespoons black pepper

2 tablespoons garlic powder

2 tablespoons onion powder

2 tablespoons chili powder

1 tablespoon cayenne pepper

1 teaspoon dried mustard

1.   Place all the ingredients in a small bowl and mix until well blended.

2.   Store in a cool area away from light in an airtight jar or sealable plastic bag.

Poultry Seasoning

Prep time: 15 minutes | Cook time: 0 minutes | Makes ¼ cup

1 teaspoon ground sage

1 teaspoon ground thyme

1 teaspoon ground marjoram

1 teaspoon rosemary leaves

1 teaspoon celery salt

½ teaspoon smoked paprika

½ teaspoon onion powder

½ teaspoon ground nutmeg

¼ teaspoon black pepper

1.   Place all the ingredients in a small bowl and mix until well blended.

2.   Store in a cool area away from light in an airtight jar or sealable plastic bag.

Garlic and Oregano Rub

Prep time: 15 minutes | Cook time: 0 minutes | Makes 1¼ cups

1 cup kosher salt

6 tablespoons garlic powder

1 tablespoon onion powder

5 tablespoons dried oregano

3 tablespoons black pepper

3 tablespoons minced dried parsley

1.   Place all the ingredients in a small bowl and mix until well blended.

2.   Store in a cool area away from light in an airtight jar or sealable plastic bag.

Mustard Vinegar Sauce

Prep time: 5 minutes | Cook time: 6 to 10 minutes | Makes 4 cups

2 cups ketchup

¾ cup cider vinegar, or to taste

½ cup Dijon mustard

½ cup dark beer

1½ teaspoons hot red pepper

1 teaspoon freshly ground black pepper

1 teaspoon sugar

1 teaspoon onion powder

½ teaspoon coarse salt (sea or kosher), or to taste

1.   Place all the ingredients in a heavy saucepan and whisk to mix. Simmer until thick and richly flavored, 6 to 10 minutes, whisking often. Correct the seasoning, adding vinegar or salt to taste: The sauce should be tangy and sharp.

Shrimp with Dill 92
Skirt Steak with Mango 55
Smoked Cashews 105
Smoked Chicken 68
Smoked Ham 37
Smoked Okra 23
Spareribs with BBQ Sauce 35
Spinach and Pork with Bacon 38
Spinach Hasselback Cheese Chicken 76
Squash with Butter 24
Steaks with Cheese Butter 49
Strip Steaks with Garlic and Oregano 52
Sweet and Spicy Pork 27
Sweet and Spicy Rub 128
Sweet Dry Rub with Paprika 131
Sweet Potato Chips 24
Syrupy Bacon 124
Syrupy Bacon 28
Syrupy Bacon Pig Pops 110

T
Tangy Chicken 83
Tangy Ginger Rib Marinade 129
Tangy Turkey Breast with Lime 90
Thyme Chicken Breast with Lemon 81
Tomato and Corn Salsa with Lime 109
Tomato and Cucumber Gazpacho 107

Tri-Tip Bottom Sirloin 49
Tri-Tip Roast 52
Tri-Tip Roast 53
Tri-Tip Roast 58
Tri-Tip Roast with Garlic 58
Trout with Lemon 93
Tuna Steaks 92
Turkey Breast with Garlic 85
Turkey Drumsticks 89
Turkey Drumsticks with Sugar 86
Turkey Duck and Chicken Roulade 84
Turkey Patties with Onion 88
Turkey Wings 86
Turkey with Carrot 89
Turkey with Chicken Rub 90
Turkey with Garlic 84
Turkey with Paprika 86
Turkey with Sweet Dry Rub 87

V
Vinegary Lamb Leg 62

W
Whole Turkey 85

Z
Zucchini Squash Ratatouille Salad 25